DEVELOPING A CAREER IN SPORT

GREG J. CYLKOWSKI

Mouvement Publications Inc.

i

DEVELOPING A CAREER IN SPORT

GREG J. CYLKOWSKI

MOUVEMENT PUBLICATIONS INC.
109 East State Street
Ithaca, New York 14850

Woodstock
19 Oaks Way, Gayton
Heswall, Wirral
L60 3SP England

Woorkarrim
Lot #7 Strathmore Drive
Torquay 3228
Australia

Copyright © 1988 by Greg J. Cylkowski
Production by Jim Powers, Ithaca, New York
Typeset by Strehle's/Grapevine Printing, Ithaca, New York
Printed in the United States of America by McNaughton and Gunn Inc., Ann Arbor, Michigan

ISBN 0-932391-35-6

Acknowledgements

With regard to this book, the author wishes to thank William Hertzman and National Textbook, Jack Clary and Contemporary Books, and the Women's Sport Foundation of San Francisco, Ca., for allowing Athletic Achievements to share in their statistical research of sport careers.

This book was edited by Kathleen Stauffer. She is an assistant editor with *Catholic Digest,* a national publication located in St. Paul, Minn.

This book is dedicated to those who in their own way have made this book possible:

my parents, for providing the necessary education which is the foundation of all my professional work

my grandfathers, Joseph Szalapski and Joseph Cylkowski, and my uncle William Morgantini, who shared a common interest of mine and always found the time to chat about America's favorite pastime — sports.

CONTENTS

CONTENTS

PREFACE

The growing emphasis placed on athletics, coupled with the increasing amount of leisure time the public now enjoys, have made the world of sports one of the fastest growing segments of American business. A whole new sports market evolved in the 1970s, and it largely was due to the formation of new sports leagues, expansion of franchises to untapped markets, and legislative enactments opening the door for female athletics. With the enactment of Title IX, and the increased television exposure for such non-traditional sports as tennis and soccer, career opportunities have dramatically risen in the 1980s — especially for women with career aspirations.

Watching and participating in sports has become a part of life for many sports enthusiasts. Sports is often the main topic of conversation between friends and acquaintances. For those who participate, sports serves as a rewarding form of relaxation and recreation. Since many dream of being in athletics on a daily basis, sports enthusiasts are constantly looking for a way to turn their preoccupation into a well-paying occupation.

The professional athlete has done what most sports fanatics dream of doing. He/she participates in athletics on a year-round basis and earns a living by doing it. Unfortunately, the proportion of our population qualified for this vocation, which has as average career life-span of only 4.5 years, is microscopic. But, there are other ways to be involved in sports and one need not be athletically gifted to enter. Since the world of sports has become a multi-million dollar entertainment industry, the demand today for various types of working men and women has blossomed. From the field of sports administration to exercise physiology, to the position of stadium managers to contract lawyers, the need for qualified individuals in select areas seems to be forever growing.

Contrary to public perception, positions in sports are not all glamour and, as in any other highly competitive field, the "big rewards" are not easily attainable. To achieve that dream career, requires initiative, hard work, and a certain amount of luck. Like any other profession, finding a job in sports is largely a matter not of what you know, but rather who you know. Still, the approach taken by this publication is that to the real winner, "you have to be good before you can be lucky." Quality people who are persistent will eventually be noticed, no matter what field of endeavor they are in.

The purpose of this publication is to give you pointers from someone who has been there and knows what it takes to realize personal goals. Like any advice you may render regarding your future, nothing beats the experience from someone who has already accomplished that interest. But advice can only take you so far. The bottom line here is "you" have to make it happen in your own life and decide what course of action is best for "your" situation.

As will be stated from time to time in this guide, the world of sports is a tough field to crack. Any athlete or successful sports administrator will tell you that sports demands much from its people, but the rewards can be substantial for those who are willing to stick it out and pay the price.

It has been said that there are three kinds of people in the world: those who watch it happen; those who wonder what happened; and those who make it happen. Whichever category you fall in will determine the success you will experience with this guide.

CHAPTER 1

WHY A CAREER IN SPORT

It's five minutes before the start of the Super Bowl. Even though you find the pre-game show interesting, you can't wait for the kick-off . . .

. . .You're one of the fifty thousand cheering fans. You can't decide if you want the manager to shorten his talk on the mound and let the pitcher throw, or if you want the conversation to go on and give the ace right hander more time to settle down . . .

. . .The center leaps high, grabs the defensive rebound, lets loose a bullet of a pass. It's caught by the quick forward, who puts it up from fifteen feet out. Two more points. Now we're down by three . . .

. . .What is the darn coach saying in the dressing room? Intermission is lasting too long. Why don't they come back on the ice for the third period and break this scoreless tie . . .

. . .You go to school or to work. That's O.K., but when you go to a game or watch one on television — that's excitement. You're lucky if your girlfriend or you wife likes it too. Maybe that's partially why you get along so well. When you get the paper you open to the sports section first. You can't wait for the television weatherman to finish his forecast so you can get the latest scores.

Let's face it. You're a sports fan. Some, who don't understand, even call you a "sports addict."

Often you think about how great it would be to actually work for a team or athletic organization. You're discouraged by comments like "Only ex-athletes get front office jobs," or "You have to be the boss' son to get a job with the team." While the ex-athlete does get priority and the owner's child can have the job if he wants it, the fact remains that with all all the new teams and franchises, there just aren't enough ex-athletes or owners' children qualified to fill the growing number of athletic organization positions.

But not all sports related careers are related to athletic organizations. As you read further into this guide, you will realize that it is going to require a great deal of imagination and an ability to let your dreams flow to find your niche in sports. For instance, let's assume that you've been a dedicated gymnast after school while also being an organic chemistry whiz academically — you could conceivably be the U.S. Olympic team's physical therapist, rehabilitating injuries and mending gold medal careers at the same time. Or if communications skills are your forte with a nose for news and a batting average of .465 on your college or amateur team, you may wind up with Joe Garagiola holding past-game interviews at the 1995 World Series. You don't have to be a youthful student much less be pursuing a career for the first time to realize your dreams. Consider this, if you are a highly organized horse fanatic with fifteen years financial-consultant experience, yo possibly could step in and manage the racetrack at Gulf-stream. And what better way for a marathoner with the patience of a research scientist to contribute to future runners than by developing the ultimate shoe as a biomechanical engineer.

These dreams and fascinations are not as farfetched as you may think. But if you allow others to discourage you and forbid your creativity to manifest itself, you could be passing up the opportunity of a lifetime.

All over the world people are preoccupied with sports. Millions of dollars are spent preparing Olympic teams to win as much glory as possible. In many countries like the United States, professional athletics has become a billion dollar enterprise supported by millions of spectators annually.

The fascination with sports in this country has reached epidemic proportions. There are hundreds of leagues in dozens of sports for students in elementary schools, junior highs, high schools, and colleges, not excluding the semi-pros along with the professional scene. In fact there are organized leagues for just about every type of person in this society. Although most of us participate in some form of recreational activity, we are also a great nation of fans. The willingness to pay money to watch athletic events has spurred perhaps the fastest growing entertainment field in our country today.

In fairness, there is one great overriding negative aspect to getting a position in sports. The field is fiercely competitive, with many hopefuls vying for a relatively few positions. Salaries are often quite low when compared to similar level positions in private industry since there is always someone who is willing to work twice as hard for half the compensation just to get a "foot in the door." But there are jobs and you may get one, if you are patient.

To assist the many people all over the United States and Canada who are interested in sports careers, Athletic Achievements has published this guide. The guide does not promise you a position but it does offer information that is not available anywhere else in publication form. Your application of the guidelines outlined in these pages will determine your success or lack of it. The guide will highlight the basic areas in athletics and will give you some helpful information in fields you may have never even considered.

It will explain the types of positions that are available, tell you where you may go for training, examine application techniques, and explore various areas of opportunities with the enclosed directory of leagues, franchises, and athletic organizations. There are jobs and although they are tough to attain, they are rewarding. Perseverance is the key to success in any vocation and with a push in the right direction, you may be on your way.

Just remember. No longer are positions in athletics and sports administration awarded only to retired professional athletes. The sports market of the future will be dominated by the creative, dedicated individual, who can foresee the trends and issues of tomorrow.

CHAPTER 2

PLAYING THE PROFESSIONAL GAME

Before any athlete can even consider pursuing any one of the most sought after professional playing careers, he/she must first address numerous intangible factors which will ultimately have an impact in deciding their professional fate. Physical talent alone will not buy a ticket to stardom since success will be an aggregate of performance variables that will be considered as a whole. A competitior's determination, game sense, performance under pressure, and resiliency are just a few of the elements that will be evaluated. Yet for other potential pro candidates who have made the grade, the inability to copoe with a grueling nuturing process, or perhaps because the demand for players in their chosen sport may not allow for financial success could force an unexpected voluntary exit from the elite ranks.

Even though the annals of sports history will exemplify heroes who possessed traits that would indicate a career such as there should never have existed, the focus of this section is not to portray the extraordinary scenario, but rather to illustrate the norm of qualifications most typically exhibited by each sport's successful performers.

In as far as the major four professional sports are concerned (baseball, basketball, football, & hockey), this publication will center its attention on the player developmental process as opposed to emphasizing the necessary physical requirements which can be attained from most any coaching guide.

Professional Baseball

The road to professional baseball is characterized by a system in which the destiny of its players may be based on considerations that are irrespective of their playing ability.

Unlike professional football or basketball whereby players are directly assigned to a team in the major circuit, the majority of pro baseball players must nurture their talents in the minor leagues. Life here will invariably test a player's character and desire as many choose to forego their dreams of notoriety on account of this factor alone.

To have a better understanding for the young ballplayer's situation, it should be pointed out that most minor league franchises are located in small remote communities that require continuous and extensive travel for league play. The daily allowances for travel and living accommodations are kept to a minimum in order for the franchise to remain financially solvent. In fact most minor league teams will operate on the revenue they generate from spring training's increased attendance when the parent club plays exhibition contests in their home ball parks.

Life can become extremely boring and at times unfulfilling in the junior circuit. George Brett of the Kansas City Royals recalls the most valuable lesson he learned in the minor leagues.

"Baseball was the most important thing in my life and I was determined not to spend too many years in the minors. You have to keep yourself motivated by setting goals higher than what you are currently doing. As soon as you get too satisfied, you're ripe for another trip down to the minors or even a lower level within the minor leagues."

The outlook for baseball remains competitive with salaries ranging from $700 a month for minor leaguers to a yearly average of $412,000 per player in 1987.

Since there is little money to be made in the minors, young players are encouraged to wait until their skills are better developed and are in greater demand. Securing a contract several years out of high school will ultimately result in a higher salary as opposed to signing at a tender young age despite the "Bonus Baby" incentives.

Collegiate baseball is fast becoming the more recommended route in which to enter the professional market considering that it presents an additional opportunity to receive a free education. Many colleges, especially in the Sun Belt regions are providing exceptional experience by playing anywhere between 60-90 games in the spring alone while at the same time keeping the amount of travel to a minimum.

The only drawback with participation in collegiate baseball is that hitters may sometimes face inferior pitching since most solid throwers are usually drafted and signed immediately out of high school.

For those baseball enthusiasts who are neither academically inclined nor feel their skills need further polishing before testing the "big league" market, another option would be to compete in one of the Mexican or Central American winter leagues. Many parent franchises assign their draftees or even cooperatively trade players with these foreign instructional leagues to better evaluate or nurture marginal prospects.

Professional Basketball

Pro basketball can be paralleled to pro football in the fact that the type of player drafted by the franchises may very well be based on the needs and coaching philosophy of each individual team. However, the one main difference with basketball in comparison to other sports is that physical size is nearly irreplaceable no matter how much success is exhibited in the other performance variables.

All basketball players should be good shooters but even though scorers and slam-dunk artists sell tickets, it is the player who will play both ends of the court — offense and defense — with equal intensity who will be awarded a college scholarship and signed to a professional contract.

Red Auerbach, former Boston Celtic coach, has this to offer young players. "Teams are successful when their players excel defensively. Therefore let it be a lesson to young players to emphasize and work on defensive skills from the very beginning. Scoring is important, but the player who plays tough defense despite not scoring as much or being recognized for flamboyant play will find a spot in the NB if the other skills are there."

The future of professional basketball has many financial concerns for both the sport and the player. Roster sizes are limited, but average playing salaries in 1986 were over $500,000 per year, while attendance figures have continued to fall in recent times. Amazing enough though, the approved expansion franchises beginning in 1988 were purchased for a record $32.5 milion each. It appears that the escalating costs associated with the NBA has yet to reach a ceiling!

Professional Football

With professional football fast becoming the national pass-time in America, it is no wonder that the overwhelming dream of most young athletes is to play in the Super Bowl.

The outlook for playing professional football as well as the financial structure has not changed drastically in the past few years despite the emergence of the now defunct USFL and expanded roster limites in the NFL. This is so because the salaries of these additional players are marginal when compared to the overall player compensation structure. First year players in the NFL can expect a starting salary of no less than $50,000 annually which includes an excellent retirement plan after 5 years. Playing in the CFL in Canada has always remained an option but unfortunately the contract offerings are not nearly comparable to those seen in the United States.

It should be pointed out that with the recent crackdown on anabolic steroids, the now disproportionate size of football players may return to the once smaller and agile athlete. This will allow for a more "rounded" athlete to succeed at positions that have more recently been restricted to the "biggest of the big." Even though much can be said for the player who is able to compensate for a lack of playing ability with the aforementioned performance factors, the fact remains that there is no substitute for talent, especially in the skill position.

Due to the larger roster sizes, professional football has the luxury of adding 200 new rookies from the college ranks each year which is higher than any other professional sport. Keep in mind though that the average playing career in football in only 4.5 years as compared to higher levels of longevity experienced in other sports. It is no wonder than that pro football's #1 overall draft pick in 1986, Bo Jackson of Auburn, chose the more secure & stable confines of professional baseball in which he was also drafted.

Professional Hockey

What it takes to make it in professional hockey is summarized best by ex-Philadelphia Flyer star Bobby Clarke, "be where the puck is. Hockey, says Clarke, is 75% mental and 25% physical." In other words, hockey players, much like defensive backs in football, need to have that 6th sense known as instinct. If a player lacks this ability and becomes totally dependent on his natural skills, it is doubtful that he will have an elongated pro career.

Another key element deemed necessary to a successful career is courage. Says Boston Bruins general manager Harry Senden, "We look for courage and not the type of aggressiveness needed to fight. A player needs courage to go after the puck or keep it when he knows he is going to get checked."

The demand for good hockey players is exceeding the supply at this time," says Harry Sinden. "A player can come into the pros and make the parent franchise within 2 years. If it doesn't happen for him in that time, chances are it may never happen at all on a full-time basis."

College hockey is turning out more professional players than ever before with many of them stepping right into the NHL. This trend was unheard of a decade ago when the last level of amateur competition before the pro ranks was the Junior A leagues in Canada. There is still some debate whether or not collegiate hockey is on the same level as Junior A, but the advantage seen by pursuing the collegiate route is the ability to receive an education necessary for life after hockey as well as still being highly visible to all the professional scouts.

Minor league hockey like minor league baseball can be very trying and demanding of its aspiring youngsters. The living and travel accommodations, not to mention the pay scale at this level, will test the fortitude of any individual. This "proving ground" is certainly no place for the insecure or timid individual.

Upon arrival into the NHL, players will receive salaries from 50,000 to as much as 175,000 per year upon of course the round in which they were drafted. Realistically speaking, unheralded rookies can expect a salary in the neighborhood of 30,000 for the first couple of seasons in the minors with bonuses occurring as they progress in the franchise.

Golf

To the amazement of many golf enthusiasts, there is a considerable process that one one must complete before being called a golf pro. The Professional Golf Association (PGA) organizes two programs, one for those who wish to become club professionals, and the other for those who will spend many of their early years on the tour.

For nearly a decade the PGA has been running an Apprenticeship Program that essentially teaches individuals how to become pro golfers. Included in the curriculum are courses in business management, practical knowledge in becoming a director of a golf club, and instruction to play a highly competitive game of golf. For men, it is translated into a score of 151 for 36 holes over a 6000-yard test course, or 163 for 36 holes over a 7200-yard course; for women, it is shooting 161 over the 6000-yard course and 175 over the 7200-yard layout.

Upon completio of this test, perspective golf pros have 6 years to become eligible for PGA membership. During this period of time several important criteria are needed before application. Credit references, experience inthe sport itself, completion of an oral test, and an examination on subjects such as teaching and merchandising are areas of substantial concern.

The specialization seen in golf today was neither required or available to young golfers in years past. Barbara Bell, coordinator for the PGA's Apprenticeship Program in Palm Beach Gardens, Florida, believes the best preparation for this phase is by attending a college where he/she can participate ina golf program and acquire an educational degree geared toward business and sports administration. Barbara notes, "In 4 years the aspiring pro will have rounded out his/her base of knowledge. After that it means applying what has been learned through practical experience."

For those wishing to become part of the popular golf tour, there also is a breaking-in period. Besides attending one of the approved tour schools held in a different region of the country each year, a player must qualify in a regional competition and later compete against other equally enthusiastic amateurs. It is not unusual for players to return 3 or 4 times before finally attaining a tour card. Even then, pros must take additional courses given under the auspices of the Association of Touring Pros (ATP), the governing body for the regular tour players.

If that isn't enough, even tour players must stay active in various phases of the game and must accumulate enough credits over a period of time to maintain their cards.

The process for women may vary somewhat as they may attend a qualifying school in Colorado Springs for a week-long seminar including a required execution of golf skills and successful completion of a written examination on the U.S. Golf Association's rules of golf. Normally only 8 women a week with USGA handicaps of 3 or less are eligible to attend.

The outlook for tour pros is good, but very competitive with yearly earnings on the 10 month tour varying from $10,000 to $500,000. Personal expenses may exceed $25,000 making it nearly mandatory to have a sponsorship. As far as local pro golfers residing at golf clubs, the outlook remains very goof for both men and women.

Famous PGA tour competitor Chi Chi Rodriguez puts golf into its perspective with this advice, "If an aspiring golfer cannot consistently score 67 over 6 months on a 6000 yard course, then he has no business competing with the pros on the PGA tour."

Listed below are the organizations which may provide additional insight into a professional golf career.

The professional Golfer's Association of America
804 Federal Highway
Box 12458
Lake Park, FL 33403

PGA Tour Office
100 Nina Court
Ponte Vedea, FL 32082

Ladies Professional Golf Association
1250 Shoreline Drive Suite #200
Sugarland, TX 77478
(713) 980-5742

Men's Professional Golf Tour
1137 San Antonio Road Suite E
Palo Alto, CA 94303
(415) 967-1305

Bowling

the Professional Bowlers' Association, like golf, has several pre-requisites that must be met before joining the tour. Both women and men must be a minimum of 18 years of age as well as being a high school graduate. Men must establish an average score of 190 during the two most recent seasons in an accredited league that has at least a 66 game schedule while women with a similar schedule, must maintain an average of 175. These scores must be verified by the American Bowling Congress (ABC).

Applicants must secure endorsements from 3 PBA members besides submitting character references. Once an application and a fee of $75.00 have been accepted by the PBA commissioner, future pros will be eligible to compete in any of the 35 national tournaments with a national membership or compete in the over 100 events regionally with a regional membership.

The outlook for professional bowlers remains good, but a sponsorship is advisable considering personal expenses may run as high as $20,000 annually. The pro tour has a 10-month season with earnings ranging anywhere from 0-$100,000 on the average.

For further information contact:

American Bowling Congress
5301 South 56th Street
Greendale, WI 53129

Professional Bowlers Association
1720 Merriman Road
P.O. Box 5118
Akron, Ohio 44313

Women's Professional Bowling Association
205 W. Wacker Drive Suite #300
Chicago, IL 60606

Ladies Pro Bowlers Tour
7171 Cherryvale Blvd.
Rockford, IL 61112
(815) 332-5756

Tennis

The professional world of tennis is divided into two career paths — touring pros and teaching pros. An advantage to becoming a pro in tennis as far as enthusiasts are concerned is the ease in attaining pro status without the intense schooling and course study.

Since touring pros live a life of notoriety and receive a more elaborate income, it is obvious why this is the more popular of the two. Touring pros first compete on the local or district level, advance to a sectional ranking, and based on that ranking and their ability to win, receive a national ranking. Many players accomplish their rankings as juniors while others develop their skills at the intercollegiate level where the pressures aren't as intense and the coursework they are studying may later prove to be invaluable. This added educational background may provide the difference to securing a position if an individual may choose to become a club pro or director once the playing days are over or if touring pro status is never achieved.

In any case, if a player cannot acquire a ranking on the local or regional level, the chances of being ranked nationally and making the tour are nill. Also, once a player does accept money in tournament play, that individual will be classified as a professional and may never revert back to amateur status.

The U.S. Pro Tennis Association governs the procedures in becoming a teaching pro. The player must be proficient as both a player and instructor. Future pros must successfully complete a 2-day test which includes demonstration of the varied tennis shots as well as expertise in teaching both private and group sessions. The final phase involves a 25-page written test with the final application requiring both employment and sponsorship references.

The future for tennis pros in both tracks is wide open considering the growing popularity of private clubs and the need for new talent on the pro tour. Unfortunately, the tennis scene is very competitive with salaries for touring pros ranging from 0-$1 million. Expenses may accumulate anywhere from $10,000 to $100,000 yearly which makes touring without a sponsorship at the start prohibitive.

Life at the local country club or tennis center may not always be so lucrative. Administrative positions usually begin with salaries in the mid-teens with the major thrust of income being received through private lessons which vary from $18.00 to $60.00 per hour.

The following schools certify potential instructors and are considered to be the foremost programs of their kind.

Vic Braden's U.S. Tennis Academy
P.O. Box 438
Trabuco Canyon, CA

Dennis Van Der Meer's Tennis University
2150 Franklin Street Suite 580
Oakland, CA 94612

Applications and further information can be obtained from the following:

U.S. Tennis Association
51 East 42nd Street
New York, NY 10017
(212) 949-9112

U.S. Pro Tennis Association
Colony Beach and Tennis Resort
1620 Gulf of Mexico Drive
Longboat Key
Sarasota, FL 33548
(813) 383-5555

Youth Tennis League
1701 Vardalia
Collinsville, IL 62234

Women's Tennis Association
1604 Union Street
San Francisco, CA 94123
(415) 673-2018

Miscellaneous Sports

Many other opportunities exist in the world of sports. Unfortunately, many of these professions are short-termed, part-time, or even struggling to maintain an existence.

To become more informed on the possibilities and requirements of becoming a professional in these sports, it will be necessary to contact the office addresses listed.

Auto Racing

With the latest technology involving computerized testing and aerodynamic engineering the car buff must be couple driving skill with mechanical specialization. There always will be auto races keeping the outlook somewhat bright. Personal expenses become exorbitant once again requiring the need of a sponsorship. Winnings may vary from merchandise to $500,000 a year.

Stock car enthusiasts contact: NASCAR
National Headquarters
Daytona Beach, FL
(904) 256-0611

Indy-type racing write: U.S. Auto Club
4910 West 16th Street
Indianapolis, IN
(317) 247-5151

Bodybuilding

The field is fast becoming a fitness fad that could ultimately produce financial rewards. This very competitive sport holds approximately 4 major events a year and is open to both men and women. Most earnings will come from guest lecturing and posing as most bodybuilders will need a major sponsor to cover personal expenses. There is undoubtedly a greater amount of personal satisfaction involved than financial rewards in this worldwide pastime.

International Federation of Bodybuilders
P.O. Box 937
Riverview, FL 33569
(813) 677-5761

Boxing

Even though in the past two decades boxing has never overcome its tarnished professional image that has depleted spectator interest, there still will always be a demand for the major title bouts. Most young boxers blossom from locally sponsored club programs which many times can lead to spots on the A.A.U. and the Olympic teams that compete internationally.

Finding a sponsor to fund boxing training is difficult unless you happen to be a national contender. Despite a growing new audience, it doesn't appear that boxing will ever be financially profitable for the average fighter.

Since the boxing world has been associated with many unethical practices which have created much apprehension in the minds of many aspiring boxers, it is in the best interest of a young boxer to check carefully with their state athletic commission to identify the names of accredited trainers and managers before they enter into any long-term contracts.

The best route to beginning a boxing career is to contact a local Golden Gloves chapter by writing:

Golden Gloves Association of America
8801 Princess Jeanne NE
Albuquerque, NM 87112

International Veteran Boxers Assoc.
94 Cresent Ave.
New Rochelle, NY 10801

Horse Racing

This "sport of kings" divides its expertise into two forms — harness racers and jockeys. Both specialists will require a sound knowledge of breeding, training, and veterinary practices along with proven riding experience.

Jockeys are seen to rise from the ranks of serving as a stable hand, to that of an exerciser, to an apprentice, and eventually to a jockey. This very competitive art of jockeying and harness racing is still male dominated and is professionally limited due to the small number of tracks and the many gambling restrictions found around the country. A maximum body weight of 110 pounds is allowed, but even more important is the knack of guiding a thoroughbred around a race course if one is to even contemplate such a career.

Both standard breed drivers and jockeys must be 16 years of age and pass a driver's exam. Earnings for jockeys will be double to that of harness racers usually in the scale of $15,000 to $200,000 for the circuit season. Personal expenses will vary but are many times picked up by the horse's owner.

For further information contact:

United States Trotting Association
750 Michigan Ave.
Columbus, Ohio 43215
(614) 224-2291

Women's Jockey Association
6075 Franklin Ave., Suite 070
Hollywood, CA 90028
(213) 705-0344

Ice Skating

In terms of time spent training and financial investment, no other sport will require the sacrifice and commitment of its participants to only have them aspire to a limited number of professional opportunities. The serious amateur figure skater will spend on the average $6,000 a year for lessons, ice rental, and equipment, not to mention the costs of travel for competitions. Those skaters wishing to compete at the national and Olympic levels will be required to train year round, many times 4-6 hours per day.

The outlook for show skating has not changed over the past decade in which males and females are equally in demand. Earnings for a 40-44 week professional tour, which many times does not include room and board, will vary from $15,000 - $25,000 for line and background skaters, to $25,000 to $100,000+ for soloists and guest appearing Olympic champions. With a shortage of male participants at the amateur level, the road to performing professionally is much easier to attain than it is for females.

Local ice rinks and figure skating clubs are the starting grounds for those interested in this year-long sport.

Many competitors choose to become skating pro instructors once they have attained their highest level of amateur status. These teaching pros will receive upwards of $25.00 to $30.00 for individual hourly sessions. To date, there are no prerequisites or requirements in becoming a teaching pro.

To learn more about amateur skating and its many associations, contact:

ISIA
Ice Skating Institute of America
1000 Skokie Blvd.
Wilmette, IL 60091
(312) 256-5060

PSGA
Professional Skaters Guild of America
P.O. Box 5904
Rochester, MN 55903
(507) 281-5122

USFSA
United States Figure Skating Association
20 1st St.
Colorado Springs, CO 80906
(303) 635-5200

The two most prominent companies that sponsor skating shows are as follows:

Holiday on Ice
3201 New Mexico Ave. NW
Washington, DC 200016
(202) 364-5000

Ice Capades
6121 Santa Monica Blvd.
Hollywood, CA 90038

14

Raquetball

The sport of raquetball peaked in popularity in the late 70's and early 80's. Though the outlook for competing in the 15 major tournaments a year remains good, most players cannot sustain the career on a full-time basis.

Earnings may vary from $1000 to $60,000 annually and as seen in so many other sports, a sponsorship is necessary to afford the many travelling and touring expenses.

For further information, contact:

Women's Professional Raquetball Association
1 Erieview Plza
Cleveland, Ohio 44114
(216) 522-1200

United States Raquetball Association
4101 Dempster Street
Skokie, IL 60076

Rodeo

The rodeo scene has recently gained popularity in several regional areas of the country and with salaries rising sharply, it's no wonder why the sport has become even more attractive to its performers. It's not unusual for the top male riders to earn in the $100,000 a year range while female performers may exceed $60,000 a year for the 600 plus events. Personal expenses may vary from $5,000 to $30,000 annually, but with a total yearly purse exceeding $2 million in both indoor and outdoor shows, the outlook for future riders remains good.

To learn more about the rodeo life contact:

Professional Rodeo Cowboys Association
2929 West 19th Ave.
Denver, CO 80204

Women's Professional Rodeo Association
8909 NE 25th Street
Spencer, OK 73084
(405) 769-5322

Skiing

Professional skiing, both men's and women's, is limited to a select few. With a very short season and only nine events a year, earnings will rarely exceed $50,000 unless endorsements or exhibitions are utilized to increase financial renumerations.

Sponsorship by ski manufacturers are common keeping the yearly personal expenses ranging from $6,000 - $15,000 down to a minimum. Many touring skiiers, like tennis pros, eventually become instructors or manage their own resorts which has the potential to be financially lucrative in the west or far northeast parts of the country.

To further investigate opportunities in this sport, contact:

Professional Ski Racing, Inc.
115 East 89th Street, IC
New York, NY 10028
(212) 427-0662

Professional Ski Instructors of America
1726 Champa, Room 300
Denver, CO 80202

TRIATHALONS

Even though the popularity of triathalons has blossomed immensely in the 80s, only a very small number of triathletes can be said to be making a comfortable living competing full-time. In fact the only triathletes that have been successful at generating personal income are usually those highly touted competitors who receive honorariums to appear in "IRONMAN" contests and national triathalon events.

The sport is still in its infant stages and sponsor dollars for individual athletes as well as prize purses aren't abundant. However, this is one of the few sports in which a sincere effort is evident in establishing winnings for men and women equal. Most triathletes will survive financially by means of consulting contracts with shoe and bike companies, product endorsements, and clinic presentations.

As seen with other non-revenue producing sports, the triathlete must travel frequently to compete and even though expenses can mount substantially, sponsors and race directors do not always pick up the tab. The primary motivator for a triathalon career should be enjoyment of the activity itself, since this may be the only real payoff.

To become a part of this fast growing sport, contact:

TRI-FED/USA
P.O. Box 1963
Davis, CA 95617
(916) 753-2828

ASSOCIATION OF PROFESSIONAL TRIATHLETES
25108 - B Marguerite
Parkway 209
Mission Viejo, CA 92692
(714) 432-8226

UNITED STATES TRIATHALON SERIES
P.O. Box 1438
Davis, CA 95617
(916) 758-9868

*A $10.00 membership fee will allow you access to events, clubs, and training camps in your area.

Soccer

Soccer is currently in a state of flux in the United States. Though its popularity continues to grow at the youth and high school levels, the game has not caught on in the professional market. Indoor soccer though has been accepted largely due to its smaller surface for increased scoring, but still is dominated by foreign performers.

Many promoters feel the American public cannot relate to supporting foreign stars while others attribute a lack of intererst to television's inability to market the product on the air.

The outlook remains bleak with current salaries averaging in the $20,000's. For those who are young enough to weather the growing pains, the best route would be to play collegiately and possibly travel abroad.

Surfing

There is little hope that this activity will ever reach full-time professional status. Those who have sponsors may win as much as $15,000 a year, but with little national or even local interest, professionals or enthusiasts should view this sport as a possible pastime.

Contact:

Professional Surfing International
5545 Taft Avenue
La Jolla, CA 92037
(714) 459-6294

American Surfing Association
Box 342
Huntington Beach, CA 92648

Waterskiing

Like its water counterpart surfing, waterskiing provides for excellent entertainment, but not as a full-time career. Most events are invitational tournaments in which the purse size relagates yearly winnings to no more than $12,000. Expenses will usually outweigh the prize money therefore requiring a sponsor.

For further details contact:

American Waterskiing Association
P.O. Box 191
Winter Haven, FL 33880
(813) 324-4341

Volleyball

Though the jury is still out on whether or not the new MVL women's professional volleyball league will remain a viable entity, the Pro Beach Volleyball Series on the other hand is fast becoming a viable spectator sport.

The tour features 26 stops in 1988 with $600,000 in prize money. Even though sponsors are readily becoming involved due to this dream market of participants & spectators who are young, free spending, affluent adults, at this point it is still ill-advised to consider this sport lifelong career endeavors.

For more information, contact:

United States Volleyball Association
557 4th St.
San Francisco, CA 94107

CHAPTER 3

COACHING

"There are two kinds of coaches
those who have been fired,
and those who are going to be fired."

Bum Phillips
Fired Coach - Houston Oilers
New Orleans Saints

Coaching is said to be rewarding, challenging, and self-fulfilling. It's also said to be exhausting, nerve-racking, and thankless. Although the coaching field is not for everyone, a variety of coaching opportunities exists to meet the philosophy and needs of each aspiring "teacher of sports" ranging from those of a volunteer, recreational nature, to the ranks of a full-salaried professional mentor.

Coaches, especially at the amateur and high school levels, are considered to be educators foremost in their coaching duties. John Wooden, former coach of the UCLA basketball program, put it into perspective by stating, "I'm a teacher of life first and then a coach, whatever that is." For those of you who are pursuing a coaching career with ambitions of attaining legendary status, wealth, and notoriety, you would be ill-advised to continue any further. Since only a minute percentage of coaches will ever reach such high status, it would be safe to assume that the greatest rewards that you will probably receive will be the satisfaction of teaching and working with young people.

Coaching at any level is a "people handling business," almost art-like in its application of getting the most out of every player. In addition to needing to be well versed in the technical and strategic aspects of the sport itself, coaches must be proficient in directing a diverse group of individuals toward a common goal. Accomplishing this goal becomes complicated, considering the many interpersonal differences, attitudes, disconcerting materialistic values, or career distractions that may exist within the team.

With the recent publicity on the extensive use of alcohol and mind-altering drugs now prevalent throughout sports, a new dimension has been added to the already numerous roles of a coach, that of being a counselor of sports. Even though there are professional services available to organizations, which deal with such matters, many coaches choose to handle these incidences "in-house" to minimize further negative media exposure or public pressure. Coexisting and establishing a rapport with the local media on these and other controversial issues unrelated to the game itself is a vital quality exhibited by coaches who are consistently successful.

There is no one way to enter the world of coaching much less any formula to guarantee positive results or achieve upward mobility. To coach professionally or in a Division I collegiate program, it is almost a prerequisite to have been a collegiate performer in that sport. But as has been repeatedly stated throughout this book, there are no steadfast guidelines etched in granite. This is best exemplified by one-time coach of the NFL Detroit Lions, Rick Farzano, who never competed beyond his high school football days. Keep in mind, though, that he is the exception, not the rule.

unfortunately individuals who had illustrious careers as competitors are often sought after to fill coaching vacancies. It has been seen time and time again, however, that such athletes rarely become successful coaches. This in part is due to the fact that coaching and performing are two distinctly different careers. Personal interaction, communication, and teaching ability are skills essential in coaching, but not necessary in competing.

The most common route taken by most first-time coaches, but not necessarily the most realistic approach, is to enroll in a physical education program and complete a coaching certification licensure. Since physical education is the study of fitness, recreation, and leisure time, it does not offer the semblance of the competitive nature of sports. For many states, though, this is the only means of acquiring a license necessary to coach in the school systems. In any case, physical education and coaching careers should be considered separate entities not interdependent on one another.

Joe Paterno of Penn State epitomizes the non-P.E. coach. Coach Paterno received an undergraduate degree in English from Brown University with all intentions of attending law school. Thirty years later he is still guiding the Nittany Lions. Paterno also illustrates how coaches who stay or are given the opportunity to be with their teams for long periods of time usually experience the highest degree of success in motivating their players to perform at maximum efficiency.

But even coaches such as Paterno who have established their reputations among the elite of their profession are now finding that the awe and respect that they once commanded is diminishing. Players of old who competed for "love of game" have been replaced by a more self-centered athlete who plays for "love of money." In this age of infalted salaries, product endorsements, post-career business opportunities, and me-first attitudes (the results of pampering players from young on) have minimized the possibility of athletes competing professionally for 10-15 years as in times past. The average playing career has been cut to only a few short years as athletes once hungry to make it to the top have now either shifted their career priorities or are unwilling to pay the price to maintain this fantasy lifestyle. No matter what distraction is experienced by the athlete of today, the job of coaching this new breed to perform to their utmost has become even more difficult and challenging in a profession that once was concerned only with X's and 0's.

Qualities of a Successful Coach

There is no single mold that creates a successful coaching style since the most basic quality that every winning coach must learn to develop is working within the confines of his/her own personality. True leaders will not concern themselves with trends or what others are doing, but instead will dictate the style that will be copied by others.

As has already been alluded, today's coach or manager is in the the people business and must concern himself/herself with this aspect as muc as his/her technical prowess.

Some of today's most prominent mentors realize that part of the success of dealing with their players will involve establishing distance from them. On the contrary, the most common mistake made by young coaches is an attempt to win the support of the team members becoming "one of the gang." This mode of thinking can only lead to a loss of respect and control.

For a sport such as baseball or hockey, where a coach travels extensively with the team for months, maintaining the proper relationship conducive to winning may make for a somewhat lonely existence. Famed baseball manager Casey Stengel used to give his Yankees a list of saloons and watering holes and then say, "These are my places. Now you find yours." Tom Landry, the only coach in the Dallas Cowboys' existence, has been nicknamed the "plastic man" for his presumed insensitivity and aloofness. But even coach Landry has admitted that there have been times when he has felt the tremendous warmth and good feelings that transpired within a dressing room, only long to be a part of them. It is his contention that there is no room for emotion in coaching since vital decisions need to be made objectively. It is also in his belief that once you come down from the pedestal that players have put on, you'll never be able to go back up in the eyes of your team.

Paul Brown was criticized for taking a similar approach in the managing Cleveland Browns. Though Brown never socialized with his players, some of whom he had coached since high school, he always made a point to look after their needs, many times without their knowledge.

It should be pointed out here that though successful, the philosophies portrayed by both Tom Landry and Paul Brown are not the only ones that have been successful. Many coaches, due to their own personality make-up or the emotional nature of the team itself, are very involved with the lives of their players. With today's more problem-oriented athlete, the parent image may be just the antidote needed to not only straighten out the personal life of the athlete, but also to turn him or her on to being more committed and productive.

If discipline is not established throughout a team's structure, no matter what style is followed, a team has little chance of succeeding. It is mental discipline that is the foreground to the discipline of rule and order. Coaches who try to create the latter without first finalizing the former are doomed.

Evaluating Talent

In line with managing athletes is the capacity to recognize talent and then develop it to its fullest potential. Though high school coaches may never have the luxury of choosing players, collegiate recruiters must be selective in distributing sometiems limited scholarships. The evaluation of talent becomes even more critical to professional teams since the draft is the main mechanism to developing a sound franchise.

There is more involved in the evaluation process than the basic physical measurements and the scores tallied. Today coaches are seeking personal attributes that they believe are in the mold of a winner. A common practice for many coaches is to select athletes with personalities and traits similar to their own. It is felt that a certain chemistry will exist between coaches and players who function under a like framework.

With the emergence of sports psychologists and the development of sport personality inventories, many of the following personal attributes can be pinpointed in a relatively short period of time with reliable results. Cattell's 16 Personality Factors and the TAIS (Test of Attentional and Interpersonal Style) are a couple of such self-scoring profiles.

- coachability
- mental toughness
- pain tolerance
- emotional control
- leadership
- self-confidence

- responsibility
- commitment
- aggressiveness
- determination

Talent selection and evaluation of personal qualities has grown so in importance that it now rivals the need to know the technical aspects of a sport. There is also an emerging belief that many of the behavioral problems that are becoming prevelent off the field in both the collegiate and professional ranks could be avoided or minimized if the character of the athlete in question was given a thorough examination along with time trials and bodily measurements. Many of today's collegiate athletes have been found to be not mature enough or socially ready to be college students, much less be sent on road trips as representatives of the institution. The professional scene, on the other hand, has begun to provide profiles on numerous athletes that were considered to be either poor prospects to succeed or somewhat of a risk. Unfortunately many scouts closed their eyes to these intangible traits and choose to make decisions on raw physical talent alone. Today's problems in sports reflect the consequences of such decisions.

For many young athletes, development will often be determined by the coach's insistence on teaching. As for young coaches, their ability to move up the ranks will ultimately be gauged on their success as teachers and their track record in nurturing raw talent. There is no substitute for reinforcing fundamentals and teaching the "little things," no matter what the level of coaching.

The most successful head coaches are noted for surrounding themselves with assistants who are good teachers. A coach who is too insecure to have a staff of the best possible assistants shouldn't be a head coach in a team sport and, in all likelihood, won't last long in that capacity.

CHAPTER 4

SPORTS ADMINISTRATION AND MANAGEMENT

In reality sports organizations are just another business entity, and the many administrative positions within these organizations are nothing more than business positions in an athletic setting. In fact, executive staff members rarely possess a sports background, as many professional franchises intentionally do not locate their business offices near their athletic facilities in order to keep their employees' responsibilities and priorities in perspective. So for those of you who perceive a career in sports to be all hype like Sunday afternoon football, a more indepth examination of the professional administrator's role is well advised.

Though not identical in structure, sports-related positions are basically the same in their job description to corresponding positions in the corporate sector. The skills and training involved in sports finance, marketing, or public relations are no different than any other business vying for the public's entertainment dollar.

This section can only illustrate to you the general job descriptions of a typical organization, but to get a real feel about a specific interest or particular occupation and learn more about the everyday intricacies of what actually is involved, visit someone performing those tasks in the field you plan to pursue. By examining the position first hand you will be able to determine if your expectations were realistic and at the same time discover if this is truly how you want to spend your work-life. You will also find out in a hurry whether you are seriously committed to a chosen career in athletics or if your interest was nothing more than a fleeting fantasy for the glamour of sports.

You could very well find yourself using this technique of informational interviewing several times in numerous careers before you discover where your niche is. As will be mentioned time and time again, revert back to your personal inventory or keep it with you mentally in developing your goals and job selection.

It's the recommendation of this publication to do your career soul searching now before you find yourself in that disillusioned position trap which could lead to permanent job dissatisfaction.

Professional Sports Administration

The majority of sports positions will be of an administrative nature. Professional sports administration can be divided into two areas: 1) the governing agencies of an entire sport — which would include the commissioner's office and 2) the team's front offices themselves. Unlike collegiate and amateur sport where the emphasis is geared towards participation and education (though many critics may hold this statement to be a lost myth), every professional team is run like a business whereby the bottom line is profit and winning, and not necessarily in that order.

Front offices will vary from sport to sport. A typical major league baseball team may staff as many as twenty positions while an NBA basketball franchise is capable of having its entire operation run by five administrative members. These varying numbers of office personnel are determined by the club's priorities and the number of support staff it will require for each department to accomplish its task. Some franchises feel a greater need to bolster such areas as community relations or promotional ad campaigns while other organizations may split these positions under one title. An NFL football club, which faces near sellouts each Sunday, can be content with only one ticket manager to run its sales campaign. On the other hand, an NBA basketball team which neither has the attendance or television revenue ($16 million annually for each NFL club) may be forced to hire a marketing and promotions specialist to assist in the sales of tickets which represents the franchise's main source of income.

Professional sports aministration is the toughest of all facets of sports to break into not only because of the small staffs, but also, as an example, when the need arises to replace or hire an individual such as a public relations or marketing specialist, such positions will usually be filled by leaders in the business world who have had as many as 20 years experience at their profession.

The basic positions in a typical front office along with a review of their responsibilities are as follows:

Executives: Team Presidents & General Managers

In today's professional sports scene, the team president is representative of someone who has invested the most money in the franchise or has been selected as president by a group of investors. Many of these executives have little knowledge of their respective sport, and by not knowing the many idiosyncracies of the business, they are not doing a justice to the parent franchise. Fortunately this older breed of administrators is slowly being phased out of the marketplace by trained, qualified members who are also aware of each sport's nuances.

The pinnacle of success for most administrators is that of general manager. The general managers of times past consisted of former players and coaches while the new breed have become more skilled in finance, promotions, and labor negotiations, leaving the involvement of player development to the director of team personnel. In many cases the GM has both team and corporate responsibilities and represents the link between the field manager (or coach) with the owners. General managers more than likely rise through the organizational ranks, possibly with a minor league team, and many times will have past playing and coaching experience.

The general manager who will succeed in the coming years will be able to deal with the always-present labor problems, understand and utilize the complexities of cable television and marketing, be knowledgeable on the most productive monetary investments, and have a feel for the changing trends that will affect the team's success.

General managers will average approximately $75,000 per year depending upon the sport itself and the responsibilities involved.

Business Manager

In many organizations if the general manager is not a strong business administrator, the business manager will become the general manager's major asset. A business manager rarely possesses an athletic background but must be well-versed in all aspects of business operations. Some of the basic responsibilities will include personnel staffing, concession bidding, financial accounting, team travel, security at events, and coordination of daily business transactions. During the team's competitive season, a 7-day work week is not uncommon.

Most of the higher management positions to be mentioned will require an undergraduate degree in business administration with an emphasis in finance and accounting. Business managers are compensated in the neighborhood of $20,000 to $40,000 annually and can expect to experience continued job security.

Traveling Secretary

Though many teams require their business managers to handle all out-of-town arrangements, almost all major league baseball and some professional football teams rely on specialists to handle this area. Traveling secretaries must travel anywhere the team competes to coordinate all travel arrangements, transportation, and living accommodations. An outgoing and patient personality is essential in this position when considering the amount of player grievances one must listen to on the road especially after a loss. A background as a travel agent would be most helpful here, but is not required.

Somewhat on the lower end of the salary scale, traveling secretaries will earn approximately $18,000 to $25,000 annually with little upward mobility possible within the organization.

Director of Public Relations

Public relations is fast replacing the term publicity on many team organization charts. The director of public relations may have other titles and responsibilities that fall within this position depending upon the needs within the organization. These titles may include director of media events, director of community relations, communications specialist, or possibly even director of promotion and advertising. The sports public relations person deals primarily with the print and electronic media, which, as Ted Haracz, who has held the job at Purdue University and with the Chicago Bears notes, ". . . makes us more accurately an information service than a public relations department."

This position can many times "make" or "break" a newly established franchise especially when dealing with the media. Public relations specialists' responsibilities will vary by organization but will usually coordinate all press activities, media campaigns, news releases, and attempt to create a positive team image in the eyes of the public. All publications, photographs, guides, and programs are filtered through this office. It is not uncommon for promotional campaigns to fall under the public relations umbrella if an organization does not have an advertising or marketing specialist. The Minnesota Twins of the American baseball league are an excellent example to the importance of special events as their team reached an all-time attendance high in 1985 by sponsoring the most promotions or "gimmicks" of any team in baseball.

Public relations is one of the most exciting yet pressure-packed positions in any athletic or corporate setting. Strong communication and journalistic skills are a must with a savvy to speak and represent the club in front of large audiences. No one ever enters the PR field directly, corporate or sportswise, but instead must serve in some intern or assistant capacity learning the position from the ground floor up. Many PR directors perform similar positions for as long as 20 years before securing the role of PR director.

Entry level public relations positions will have salaries in the mid-teens while PR directors are handsomely compensated for in the range of $40,00 to $60,000 annually.

Ticket Manager

A director of ticket sales may also serve as a marketing director involved with group sales much in the capacity as a promotion assistant. The "people" aspect of the job is important since ticket personnel are the only personal link between the public and the team. This becomes even more apparent when considering the amount of complaints that must be listened to concerning seat location, prices, or even the way the team is playing.

A knowledge of computers, an ability to keep accurate records as well as being meticulously organized are prerequisites to being a successful ticket manager. There is no travel and little contact with players and coaches. In fact it is not unusual for ticket personnel to rarely see their team play since their duties only begin once the patrons are seated.

The field is relatively easy to enter but the average salary range is from only $11,000 to $20,000 yearly with little chance for job enhancement or promotion.

Arena/Stadium Managers

New arenas and stadiums continue to be built in every size of city and town all over the country thus creating a need for specialists in facilities management. These executive-type positions require promotional skills foremost with little need for an intimate knowledge of sports. Success in this phase of sports management will be based on one's ability to be flexible, foresighted, and efficient in planning details since it is not uncommon for a multitude of events to be scheduled in a short period of time.

With the ever increasing popularity of concerts, conventions, and shows, multi-purpose sports facilities seek individuals who possess a promotional background in order to schedule events on a year-round basis. This concept is becoming ever prevalent due to the fact that many arenas and stadiums are public financed and must show a profit to justify their existence.

Strong management skills with a business administration degree are prerequisites for someone wishingto be a facilities director. Experience and internships are readily attainable with existing stadiums and arenas. Long hours with considerable travel in order to book major shows and attractions are commonplace in this wide open field. Compensation for a managing director in a municipal arena or stadium could be as high as $40,000 to $60,000 a year as smaller facilities managers who may be required to take on additional administrative responsibilities, may earn in the upper $20,000's.

Computer Specialists

Computers will represent the basic function of any business in the future with sports being no exception. Many professional football clubs rely on their computer banks not only in formulating team preparations, but also in establishing season ticket lists, publicity outlets, financial data, and player information.

Football utilizes computers more than any other professional sport. This should be of no surprise when considering the amount of play calling and player match-ups that are encountered in any given contest. Computers may be able to decipher tendencies or the predictabilities of an upcoming opponent in addition to being able to scout one's own team for deficiencies.

Computer programmers and specialists need not possess technical sports knowledge, but do need to be well versed in sports terminology. Since supply overshadows current demand, technicians should expect to earn slightly below the present corporate market scale considering that so many individuals are willing to accept a lower salary in lieu of working for a sports franchise.

College Sports Administration

While the professional administrative ranks usually have a higher scale of employee compensation and a more prestigious work environment, the collegiate scene on the other hand will offer better job security in addition to providing a broader base of experience for individuals wishing to advance in the sports job market.

Since collegiate athletics operates numerous sports programs for both men and women on limited budgets, many of these positions will integrate the responsibilities for several areas of expertise. This will ultimately benefit the young administrator who will acquire a more varied background and flexibility for possible future considerations. Also, with the many major sports being offered at universities for much of the calendar year, there exists an environment of continuous excitement and enthusiasm as opposed to professional sports, which may be in the spotlight for only 4-6 months of the year.

The basic administrative positions and job descriptions in college sports are virtually the same as those already mentioned in comparable roles in the professional circle. However, due to the structure and needs of collegiate sports programs, many of these similar type positions have specialized duties and tasks which are not necessary functions in a professional franchise.

Athletic Director

This position will vary according to the size and the athletic philosophy of the institution involved. Unlike the general manager in the professional ranks, the collegiate athletic director must also be a fund raiser, a politician, and a personnel administrator, yet still be a sound finance manager. If there is such a thing as an athletic director prototype, this individual would have a post-graduate degree in education or liberal arts with an accounting or business administration track record. Though it is not mandatory, most Division I athletic directors will have coaching experience which will present both credibility and a common link to the coaches that perform under him/her.

An athletic director must serve the coaches and athletes first while also taking on the role of liaison between the student body and faculty. The AD is also responsible for the department's financial status and therefore will usually answer to the Board of Regents of the college's governing body or the school president.

With the NCAA continually re-evaluating its policies and regulations, including the legal mandates involving women's sports, the AD has become a politician of sorts in establishing a cooperative relationship between men's and women's athletic departments. This becomes even more evident when it comes time to allocating limited available resources. Few universities still operate under segregated programs, but for those that do, there is a shortage of female AD's who have both an athletic and administrative background.

Since balancing the books is the very reason this position exists, the AD of the future will be a successful fund raiser. The majority of an AD's travel time will transpire during fund raising events. Depending on the needs of the program, many universities are now hiring public relation-type AD's with associate or assistant athletic directors taking on more of the administrative duties.

The perceived powers of the athletic director are not as prevalent as the average fan may think. Though many schools' AD's are allowed to hire and fire coaching staffs, it is not unusual for departments with prominent football and basketball programs to have the department's power residing within these head coaches. If this situation presides, the AD performs in nothing more than a coordinating capacity as opposed to actually performing directorship responsibilities.

This highly pressured and time consuming position can vary in salary from $30,000 annually in a Division III school, to possibly $80,000 yearly at a nationally known institution. Assistant and associate athletic directors, which will perform specific administrative functions for AD's, will earn in the range of $25,000 to $50,000 per year.

Business Manager

The business manager at the collegiate level retains a very low profile. This person may be required to coordinate all administrative functions including those of a traveling secretary. Little to no athletic knowledge is required in this position but strong accounting and finance experience is a must.

The athletic director's right-hand person will be compensated from $35,000 to $40,000 annually. Unfortunately, only the larger institutions can afford the luxury of a business manager. For those schools who do not have a business manager the AD will either assume or delegate likewsie responsibilities.

Sports Information Director

Unike professional sports, the collegiate ranks usually will not employ a public relations or marketing specialist, but instead will include those functions in the SID's job description. The SI staff will serve as a communication line between the athletic department and the media coordinating and publishing all statistics, programs, and informational news releases.

The sports information department offers excellent opportunities for entry level individuals but does not provide the environment or training needed for upward mobility within an athletic department. The sports information assistant will unlikely stay with any one SI department for more than a few years if he/she is not promoted to the program's sports information director. This constant movement allows for continuous turnover therefore creating numerous openings in the field. Strong journalistic skills, a nose for statistics, the dedication to work long hours under tight deadlines, and an ability to effectively deal with the media are prerequisites for anyone entering this line of work.

The pay scale for this high energy position will start at $14,000 for an entry level assistant to possibly $35,000 annually for a director with considerable experience at a Division I institution.

Fund Raising Director

Due to escalating costs and maximum ceiling prices already on game tickets, the concept of fund raising is steadily becoming a key factor to the financial survival of intercollegiate athletics. Contrary to public belief, collegiate athletic departments are self-sustaining and are not subsidized by student tuition fees. Therefore for budgets to increase, so must revenue.

Entry level positions in this area are one of the fastest routes to entering collegiate sports while providing an opportune chance to be involved in the total operations of a collegiate athletic program. Most fund raising directors work closely with the university's foundation, (fund development office) but depending on the demands and needs of a particular school, typical responsibilities would include donor prospecting and solicitation, alumni group organization, booster club coordination, distribution of donor benefits, and responsibility for directing out-of-town promotional trips.

Fund raising today is characterized by more than just outright cash donations as it now resembles an investment market. The sale of insurance policies, scholarship endowments, and bequests of wills are some of the methods now used to preserve collegiate athletics for the future. An additional concept that has become popular is for schools with successful basketball and football programs to require a donation for the rights to have season tickets at center court or the 50 yard line. However for schools with 85,000+ attendance figures in football, fund raising is not a priority due to the already high ticket income.

A good marketing background with a desire to work with the public are necessary attributes for someone wishing to pursue fund raising. Advanced degrees are not required as the salary range varies from a low of $14,000 for a nonexperienced entry level assistant to $35,000 annually for a seasoned director.

Academic Counselors

With the increased emphasis on academics for college athletes, a growing number of schools are adding academic to their sports staffs. Even though education is the very basis for athletes attending college, coaches many times do not have the expertise or time during the season to be informed on the progress of each individual student.

These counselors are therefore responsible to advise students academically on necessary course requirements, career decisions, and progress towards completion of a degree program. They also must keep in stride with NCAA requirements and eligibility standards and if the need arises, provide individual instruction for problem students which may result in accompanying teams for out-of-town contests.

The typical academic advisor position does not currently require post graduate work, but the trend will be for future counselors to have specialized training. It is not necessary to have been an athlete to function adequately in this capacity, but most of today's ranks are comprised of ex-coaches and administrators. The salary scale is comparable to that of an assistant football or basketball coach of $24,000 to $33,000 yearly.

Amateur Athletics

Like coaching, there are many non-profit or amateur organizations who are always seeking administrative assistance especially in fundraising abilities. Unfortunately these positions are of a part-time nature or offer low salary structures.

Recreation administration through the county or city however can offer competitive pay scales with excellent job security. Check with your local municipal personnel office for possible openings.

High School Athletic Directors

For those coaches or teachers who enjoy working with young people, becoming a high school director can be very rewarding. A typical high school AD will put in long hours usually after school in overseeing home contests, coordinating schedules, ordering equipment and uniforms, managing a staff of coaches, groundskeepers, and secretaries, and attending numerous parental booster club meetings and special interest groups.

The scope of the athletic director's duties will depend largely on the district's needs and athletic priorities. The AD's role can vary from that of a full-time position for within a total district or for one school, to possibly serving in a part-time capacity at a school along with other teaching and coaching assignments. The powers of the athletic director can be limited since most policies on discipline and participation may be mandated from the district itself.

Vacancies are scarce and are usually filled by an "in-house" staff member. The many budgeting cuts in athletics has forced many schools to merge programs or utilize an area AD for several schools.

The salary range for a full-time athletic director will usually fluctuate between $25,000 and $35,000 with part-time administrators receiving stipends in the neighborhood of $5,000.

Training & Education in Sports Administration

When applying for a position in sports administration or any other sports related field, it is not essential that the education involved come from a specialized sports institution. In many cases, positions are created requiring diverse amounts of qualifications and experience that could be acquired in a variety of institutions or business settings. As was mentioned earlier, the field of sports administration is nothing more than a business administrative role within a sports atmosphere. A good example of the expectations for an aspiring sports enthusiast is this statement from the Chairman of Madison Square Garden and President of the New York Yankees, Michael Burke: "We do not expect young people coming to the Yankees right out of college to have any technical knowledge that can be immediately applied. Rather we are eager to get young men who are bright, willing and able to apply their general talents to any number of assignments as they learn the baseball trade."

For those who have not yet started a career and for those who have time to attend classes in sports administration of a chosen field, there are universities and colleges offering courses that may make the difference in securing a position. While no school can guarantee placement in a job upon graduation, many of these institutions have outstanding success records, especially in attaining internships with major university and professional programs. The professional and collegiate ranks enjoy turning to specialized institutions since in reality the schools are doing all the screening of their future employees. The following is a list of programs that are well known throughout the country.

Durham College

The Sports Administration program is the only two-year diploma course in its kind in Canada, and remains unique in its content and approach.

This approach is not designed to develop coaches, trainers, or athletes. Instead, the program focuses its attention on the skills of the administrator who must relate to all aspects of the Canadian sports scene. Graduates may aim at many responsible positions with professional sports teams, amateur sports organizations, recreation agencies, private facilities and within the sporting goods industry.

With the very rapid development of sport, from the international to the local level, both amateur and professional, and the emergence of government support to traditionally volunteer agencies, new possibilities for full-time employment are expanding. No single educational institution other than Durham College offers a practical, skills-oriented program to satisfy this need.

Training in this program focuses upon the development of knowledge, understanding, skills and values in both functional and general administrative areas, and in specific sport related areas. The course is conducted in an atmosphere of lecture, workshop, practical assignment and discussion situations combined with extensive second year field work experience.

Third Year Program Option

An optional year may be available should demand warrant. The third year program will be offered both on and off campus through continuing education. The program will include extensive fieldwork study, student presentations, and a learning centered educational format.

Entrance Requirements

An OSSGD with year 4 English is required and preferably with Mathematics.

Direct entry admission to year 2 and year 3 will be considered based on related post-secondary education and practical experience. Individuals should be aware that this is a limited enrollment program. All students who are accepted to the program will be requested to attend an orientation-interview.

For further information regarding Durham College, contact:

Robert W. Hedley
Department Head
Administrative, Communication, & Applied Arts Division
Durham College of Applied Arts & Technology
P.O. Box 385
Oshana, Ontario Canada

(416) 576-0210, Ext. 377

St. Thomas University

St. Thomas University (formerly Biscayne College) in Miami, Florida, was the first institution to offer an undergraduate degree in sports administration. St. Thomas also offers a Master's program which places special emphasis on management and communication skills. A unique function at St. Thomas is its faculty composed of experts in various sport related fields who will lend professional counsel in seminars, internships, and independent study courses.

St. Thomas has been able to establish an internship program for its advanced students which in many cases has led to a permanent position. Typical courses offered at St. Thomas include: Current Issues in Sports, Athletic Public Communications, Arena Management, Profit Income Expenditure Factors in Athletics, and seminars and symposiums in Sports Administration.

For further information on St. Thomas' graduate and undergraduate programs, contact:

Andy Kreutzer
Director - Sports Administration
St. Thomas University
16400 N.W. 32nd Avenue
Miami, Florida 33054

(305) 625-6000, Ext. 108

St. John's University

St. Vincent's College of St. John's University in New York was the first university level school to offer a four-year bachelor's degree in Athletic Administration. According to St. John's, the administration of athletics requires well-educated, dynamic, intelligent individuals. Its program offers special training in the areas of supervision and executive management.

Courses concentrate in public and media relations, player contracts, personnel management, advertising and purchasing. An internship in some area of athletic administration is a key addition to the program. During the internship, the student will get partial on-the-job training with an athletic organization and make contacts for future employment. Being located in a city like New York which has so many teams is another plus for the St. John's program. Some of the courses offered in the program include: Legal Aspects of Athletic Administration, Current Issues in Sports, Seminars in Sports Administration, Broadcast Journalism, Public Relations, Sportswriting, Security Problems, and Financial Management.

For further information regarding this program, contact:

Dean Beglane
Athletic Administration Program
St. Vincent's College,
St. John's University
Grand Central and Utopia Parkways
Jamaica, New York 11439

(212) 990-6161

United States Sports Academy

One of the most innovative and specialized institutions for those interested in athletics is the U.S. Sports Academy. The school's graduate division has established one of the foremost programs in Sports Medicine and Sports Administration by recruiting the nation's leading figures in these fields to serve as advisors and instructors.

A key aspect of the Academy's student services is not only its ability to place applicants with positions in the United States, but also throughout the world where professional athletic expertise is lacking. Physical educators, coaches, recreation specialists, and administrators alike are encouraged to send their credentials to the Academy for the possibility of overseas employment.

The U.S. Sports Academy is very selective regarding the admission of students to its highly technical programs. For more information, contact:

Dave Voskuil
United States Sports Academy
Box 8650
Mobile, Alabama 36608

(205) 343-7700

University of Massachusetts

The University of Massachusetts of Amherst, Massachusetts offers a master's degree in Sports Studies with a related degree in Sports Administration. Sports Studies specializes in the history, philosophy, sociology and social psychology of sports. In addition to course work, students in sports administration intern with a sports organization and take courses in the School of Business Administration. A specialization in Sports Administration is also offered to undergraduates at this University.

For more information about this Sports Studies program, write:

Guy Lewis/Dept. of Sports Studies
School of Physical Education
Curry Hicks Building
University of Massachusetts
Amherst, Massachusetts 01002

(413) 545-0621

Western Illinois University

Western Illinois University has offered a master's program in Sports Management since 1972. This degree program involves the Departments of Physical Education and the College of Business at W.I.U. and includes two required courses in each discipline. Elective courses relevant to a student's career interests provide for flexibility and may include, in addition to other course work in Physical Education, courses in Communications, Computers, Educational Administration, Management, Marketing, Personnel, Psychology, Recreation and Sociology. The culminating experience of the program is an internship which generally involves one semester off-campus. Students electing the school track serve their internship in a secondary school or a college/university while those following the non-school track usually earn internship credit within a professional sports organization or in another sports related business. During the past 11 years students have served internships nationwide with 125 different institutions and organizations. Graduates of the program may be found in all areas of Sports Management including positions with the following: (organizations) Chicago White Sox, Detroit Pistons, Milwaukee Bucks, Rochester Red Wings, San Antonio Spurs, San Francisco Cow Palace, Wilmot Fitness Club; (universities) Florida International, University of Illinois — Chicago and Urbana, Maryland, Nebraska, Richmond, San Jose State, Southern California, Texas A & M, West Texas State, Witchita State.

For more information regarding this program, contact:

Dr. Beatrice Yeager
Physical Education Graduate Coordinator
Western Illinois University
Macomb, Illinois 61455

(309) 298-2103

Robert Morris College

Robert Morris College has added an exciting option to its M.S. Degree program in Business Administration — Sport Management.

The Sport Management M.S. program builds on a core of coursework in accounting, finance, quantitative methods, marketing, and business information systems. The curriculum is aimed at giving the modern sport manager insight into the application of social, legal, and business theory in the sport or recreation organization.

Internship Opportunities

This involves a field experience with a sport or recreation organization related to the student's area of interest. The following organizations are among the many who have made internship programs available to qualified sport management students.

- Pittsburgh Spirit
- Pittsburgh Penguins
- Sporting Goods Manufacturers Association
- Professional Nautilus and Fitness Center
- Off the Wall Racquetbll Ball
- Detroit Pistons
- Sewickley YMCA
- Athlete's Foot Sporting Goods
- Blesto, Inc.
- U.S. Olympic Committee
- Cleveland Cavaliers
- Eastern College Athletic Conference
- Pittsburgh Civic Arena

For additional information, write or call:

Professor Stephen Hardy, Chairman
Department of Sport Management
Robert Morris College
Narrows Run Road
Coraopolis, PA 15108

(412) 262-8302

Indiana University of Pennsylvania

Indiana University of Pennsylvania in Indiana, Pennsylvania, started a Master's Degree in Sport Sciences in 1977. Although an academic major in business or health and physical education is suggested, the program is open to any qualified graduates with a baccalaureate degree from a recognized institution.

Students may select from a variety of emphasis areas in sport management, sports information, sports communication media, and industrial fitness consultation. IUP has the only master's degree program in Aquatic Administration that is recognized by the National Aquatics Council. Graduates from these programs have enjoyed considerable success in obtaining a variety of positions in sports related careers.

An undergraduate program in Sports Administration leading to a B.S. in Sport and Physical Education (non-teaching) degree is currently awaiting approval. For further information, please contact:

Dr. James Mill, Chairman
Health and Physical Education Dept.
Zink Hall - 225
Indiana University of Pennsylvania
Indiana, Pennsylvania 15705

(412) 357-2770

Wayne State University

The Master of Arts degree in Education with a major in Sports Administration, is designed to prepare the student for a career within the broad spectrum of sports programs, sports agencies, and related organizations. Students may select from three areas of specialization: Interscholastic Athletic Administration, Intercollegiate Athletic Administration, or Professional and Commercial Sports Programs Administration.

Flexibility will be the key to individual program planning with a selection of courses from Physical Education and other sports services. An important program requirement for each student will be successful completion of an extended internship with an off-campus organization.

Applicants for admission to the graduate program should be directed to:

Dr. Vernon Gale
Division of Health & Physical Education
Wayne State University
Detroit, Michigan 48202

(313) 577-4269

Rice University

The sport management concentration at Rice is designed to familiarize the student with the operation of profit and non-profit organizations. It will provide students with an excellent foundation of management theory coupled with the practical experience of an internship.

The program offers a core of required courses that include the applications of social and business theory in the sport or recreation setting. Specialty track options allow the student to tailor special interests through a variety of electives.

For further information on this highly selective program, contact:

Dr. Kathy A. Davis
Dept. of Health & Physical Education
Box 1892
Houston, Texas 77251

(713) 527-4808

Mankato State University

Mankato State University, training site for the Minnesota Vikings of the NFL, offers the only bona fide sports management program in the upper Midwest. The master's program emphasis is geared for the student who has aspirations in becoming an athletic director. An internship is offered on campus as an assistant in the athletic department.

Courses are taken through the Department of Physical Education which also offers a specialized track in athletic training which is known nationally.

For further information, contact:

Denny Erie
Dept. of Physical Education
Mankato State University
Mankato, Minnesota 56001

(507) 389-6313

Following is a state-by-state composite listing of institutions that offer sports administration programs. In Most instances information may be obtained by contacting the Chairman of Sports Science Studies who will usually reside in the Department of Physical Education.

U—Denotes Undergraduate Program Offered
M—Denotes Graduate Degree Offered

Arizona
Arizona State University (M)
Tempe, AZ 85281

University of Arizona (U)
Tucson, AZ 85721

California
University of Southern California (M)
Los Angeles 90089-0652

District of Columbia
American University (M)
Washington, D.C. 20016

Florida
St. Thomas University (U, M)
Miami, FL 33054

Georgia
University of Georgia (M)
Athens, GA 30613

Georgia State (M)
Atlanta, GA 30303

Idaho
　Idaho State University (M)
　Pocatello, ID 83201

Illinois
　Eastern Illinois University (M)　　　　Western Illinois University (M)
　Charleston, IL 61920　　　　　　　　Macomb, IL 61453

Kansas
　Wichita State University (M)
　Wichita, KS 67208

Kentucky
Eastern Kentucky University (M)
Richmond, KY 40475

Louisiana
　Grambling State (U, M)　　　　　　　Louisiana State University (M)
　Grambling, LA 71245　　　　　　　　Baton Rouge, LA 70803

Maryland
　University of Maryland (M)
　College Park, MD 20742

Massachusetts
　University of Massachusetts (M)　　　Northeastern (M)
　Amherst, MA 01003　　　　　　　　　Boston, MA 02115

Michigan
　Central Michigan (M)　　　　　　　　Western Michigan (M)
　Mt. Pleasant, MI 48858　　　　　　　Kalamazoo, MI 49008

Minnesota
　Mankato State (M)
　Mankato, MN 56001

Mississippi
　Jackson State University (M)
　Jackson, MS 39200

New York
　Adelphi University (M)　　　　　　　C.W. Post College (U)
　Garden City, NY 11530　　　　　　　Brookville, NY 11548

　Long Island University (U)　　　　　New York State (M)
　Brooklyn, NY 11201　　　　　　　　Brockport, NY 14420

　New York University (M)
　New York, NY 10003

Ohio
　Ashland College (U, M)　　　　　　　Bowling Green State (M)
　Ashland, OH 44805　　　　　　　　　Bowling Green, OH 43403

　University of Cincinnati (M)　　　　　Kent State University (M)
　Cincinnati, OH 4521　　　　　　　　Kent, OH 44242

　Ohio State University (U, M, D)　　　Ohio University (M)
　Columbus, OH 43210　　　　　　　　Athens, OH 45701

Oregon
　University of Oregon (M)
　Eugene, OR 97403

Pennsylvania
    Indiana University of Penn. (M)
    Indiana, PA 15705

    Robert Morris College (U)
    Coraopolis, PA 15108

South Dakota
    University of South Dakota (M)
    Vermillion, SD 57069

Texas
    Rice University (U)
    Houston, TX 77001

Washington
    Washington State University (M)
    Pullman, WA 99164

Wisconsin
    University of Wisconsin (M)
    Superior, WI 54880

Wyoming
    University of Wyoming (M)
    Laramie, WY 82071

Penn State (M)
University Park, PA 16802

Temple University (M, D)
Philadelphia, PA 19104

University of Washington (M)
Seattle, WA 98105

CHAPTER 5

BUSINESS IN SPORTS

Until the mid-1960s, business and sports only flirted with the idea of becoming "big time." Now it is a rare occasion when a major corporation does not involve itself in some way with sports. Whether it be food, apparel, automobiles, or a predominating lifestyle, the central theme in advertising, marketing, sales, or purchasing will attempt to involve a sports related concept.

With the arrival of sports on the business scene, the demand has increased for those who can speak and conceptualize the ramifications of sports in application to other walks of life. Take for instance the insurance industry which has expanded its "special risk" coverage to include athletics. It has become commonplace for a football quarterback to have his arm insured or a runner to set a premium on his legs. Or how about the lawyer who handles contract negotiations and investment procedures for professional athletic clients who are now regularly having their salaries deferred for as long as a 20-year period of time for tax purposes.

Keep in mind that with each new developing sport gaining public acceptance, there will also be a need for advertising and promotion of the activity, along with a whole new line of sporting equipment that will evolve to meet the newly created interest. It therefore becomes evident that each new sports entry will ultimately increase the demand for sports related business personnel.

The point to remember here is that you don't have to be an athlete much less an avid fitness participant to be successful in a sports related business career. It would be amazing for many to discover that there are manufacturers of sports equipment who probably couldn't even demonstrate their product proficiently. Success in any business field is attained by the same disciplines and skills that are the foundation of successful retail salesmen, corporate lawyers, public accountants, and middle managers. These people will ascertain that there is no substitute for knowledge, dedication, ability, foresight, experience, and hard work.

Sporting Goods

The sporting goods industry exemplifies the need for sound business principles in a sports environment. This segment of sports is comprised of people with expertise in personnel, production, finance, marketing, sales, and research.

Individuals working in this industry need not be sports experts; in fact, those athletes who have competed utilizing the sport specific products are many times less qualified to sell or even market the equipment. The disadvantage of hiring such successful athletes may be that they already have a prejudice about equipment which may not even be within the realm of the company's product line. Therefore, the only real demand for the "athlete-specialist" is in the phase of product development and design.

Employment opportunities in sporting goods sales are increasing but not without a high turnover rate that is attributed to the exorbitant amount of traveling that may be required of the marketing representative. The two prerequisites all companies seek in prospective employees are college degrees with emphasis in business and marketing and hands-on experience. Neither of these elements may take precedence over the other unless the applicant has already established a successful sales track record with another firm.

Marketing and sales staff people will usually receive a base + commission for salary compensation. An entry level earnings figure of $13,000–$20,000 can be expected in the early stages of sales with increases and bonuses occurring rapidly as sales volume and contracts increase.

Retail Sporting Goods

With America's preoccupation with physical fitness, sporting goods retail businesses have blossomed by leaps and bounds. The general type store which stocks everything from uniforms to baseball gloves along with fitness equipment to tennis apparel still dominates the market, but a growing trend has begun to emerge with specialty outlets. These sport specific stores will feature and specialize in a one or possibly only a unique line of recreation or sports merchandise such as camping equipment, bicycles, or fitness apparatus.

No longer is the trend for retail businesses to be owned by sole proprietorship since specialization has also increased the need for regional chains to keep costs competitive. This conglomerate effect has created a whole new market for management staffs including those with expertise in promotions and sales skills. Knowledge and first hand usage of the many product lines can only enhance the success and future advancement of the retail sales person. Since new product lines are flooding the market on almost a daily basis, the retailer's education and experience with each product will better enable the purchaser to make a correct choice and become a repeat buyer.

Entrance into the retail market is not difficult considering sales staff personnel often start with rather conservative hourly salaries. For those with management aspirations, salaries will begin in the area of $14,000 with quick advancements. The retail industry is noted for its low salary structure and long hours, but with the right attitude and some capital backing, ownership of a sporting goods dealership is attainable within 5 to 10 years.

Training

Very few sporting goods retailers actually receive formal specialized training and preparation to enter this industry. However those individuals who are successful will have a strong background in sales, marketing, and business administration.

The institution that does offer a structured program designed for career work in the sporting goods industry is the University of Massachusetts in Amherst. This school has already been outlined in an earlier section for providing flexible coursework in sports facilities management, recreation, and athletic administration.

Probably the most advanced program devised in sporting goods sales and management is offered by the Minneapolis Technical Institute. The 46 week curriculum emphasizes all phases of product knowledge and salesmanship. Students attending the institute are from all educational backgrounds and the school is not restricted to first time career seekers. The Minneapolis Institute boasts a 98% placement rate within student's area of concentration.

For information or application and acceptance procedures contact:

Admissions Office
Minneapolis Technical Institute
1415 Hennepin Avenue
Minneapolis, Minnesota 55403

(612) 370-9430

Also, a good contact for possible future employment is as follows:

National Sporting Goods Association
1699 Wall Street
Mount Prospect, IL 60056

(312) 439-4000

Insurance

The insurance designated for athletes is termed "special risk." So "risky" is this field that very few independent agencies in the country even attempt to write such policies. There is one distinct advantage that comes along with writing these extremely high premiums — high income. Only sound insurance entrepreneurs with a background in the risk areas will be able to develop policies for athletes and teams or for advertisers that use athletes for endorsements. Knowledge of sports or athletics is not essential, but a feel for sports law will be invaluable.

The type of insurance policy to be dealt with is not unlike those written on the late Jimmy Durante's famous nose or Betty Grable's shapely legs. These physical features were essential to the individual's popularity and the revenue that they brought to themselves, their studios, and the many who promoted their careers.

Before writing such a policy, a special-risk coverer must develop a special sense for determining an athlete's market value by projecting proposed salaries and establishing the true existing physical condition of his/her's athlete. The insurer should also have a feel about the nature of the sport and the risks that are involved which would actually bring a rise for such a claim.

Since the insurance industry has its own method of certifying agents, it is better to contact the industry itself directly to acquire proper procedures and information.

Marketing Consultants

With increasing costs and rising salaries causing fewer sports organizations each year to show a profit, many administrators are now contracting specialists in advertising, promotions, and fund raising to assist them in creating imaginative revenue schemes. Universities and professional franchises are finding this approach of rendering the services of a consultant more cost effective than employing additional staff members since specialists can spend more time and perform more thorough evaluation for a particular need. Marketing specialists have been especially effective in the acquisition of television and radio sponsors, ticket sales, and promotion events to targeted groups.

Before franchises can be awarded or stadiums erected, marketing and feasibility studies must be completed. Marketing studies are utilized to measure a designated market for interest, potential growth such as a television market, and income diversity. A feasibility study will ensure predictions of meeting environmental standards, stadium accessibility for crowd control, and the demographics of a particular populated area.

This type of sports involvement has been attractive to the non-athletic individual who can serve in the capacity as a corporate executive and still be a part of the sports world. Degrees in business administrative with graduate studies in finance, advertising, and marketing are necessary components for developing a sound background. Most professional consultants have as many as 20-30 years of practical experience before they enter private practice, but once an associate has created an established reputation, fees for consulting services can range as high as $2,000 per day.

Advertising Agents

Sports has become a dominant theme in advertising with some of the most popular television ads dealing with past and present sports figures. Unfortunately very few agencies concentrate exclusively on sports marketing concepts considering sports advertising is not all-consuming to the buying public, as a whole.

For those entering this highly competitive field, a thorough understanding in marketing, sales, and advertising, along with creative instincts and a knowledge of sports and athletics will provide the perfect blend of working attributes. The key to success in this business is being able to tie in the athlete or sports related message with a client's product and attracting attention to it. This can only be accomplished if the agency understands the sports market and knows the strengths and weaknesses of the sports figures in relation to the product.

Tenacity, perseverance, and imagination are essentials to entering the world of advertising. It will take several years to be established within a firm, but for those who can weather the numerous payment of dues, a handsome compensation structure will begin in the $30,000's. Becoming a junior partner or assisting in volunteer campaigns are the only proving grounds for an advertising hopeful who possesses little experience.

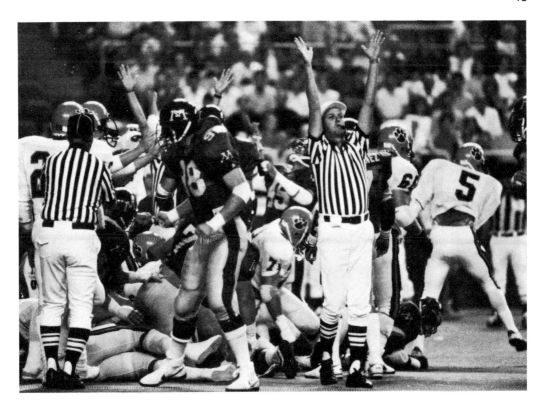

CHAPTER 6

SPECIALTY SPORTS CAREERS

Not every sports-related career can be classified under the preceding headings already mentioned. There are also other careers that will provide opportunities in sports in which some may be of the traditional nature only to not have received as much notoriety while others are relatively new and still developing.

Sports Officiating

"The best thing is to play,
the second best is to coach,
and the third best is to officiate the sport you love."

Dr. Henry Nichols
NCAA & Olympic Basketball Referee

For many years officials were the frequent target of verbal, and on occasion, physical abuse from coaches, players, and the fans. More recently a growing respect, almost admiration-like, has transpired at all levels for the men and women who make the game possible by enforcing the rules. With a more educated awareness on the importance of officials, not only is there a greater appreciation for their thankless work, but also there has been an increasing interest in becoming a member of those known as the "men in blue" or the "zebra" corps.

Most officials earn their livelihood as educators, self-employed businessmen, or in careers such as sales which have flexible hours making it possible to officiate afternoon sporting events.

While ninety-five percent of all officials serve in a part-time capacity and consider the profession more of an avocation, a select few will qualify to make it a full-time career.

The road to the professional ranks has many dues to be paid. The first phase in developing skills will be in acquiring experience at the lower levels of play. This begins by working with youth programs and the high schools eventually leading up to the collegiate conference and the minor leagues. Countless nights are spent on lonely distant highways obtaining the necessary nurturing that must take place before one may even be considered for the "big time." This often trying lifestyle should be of a major consideration when contemplating a career in officiating. Unless you are a football referee who performs only on weekends, the remainder of the officiating corps will travel extensively for months at a time. Being away from family or close acquaintances has been more than a strain on many referees' marriages and personal well being.

Officiating, like so many other occupations, requires a certain personality type as it definitely can be said that it is not for everyone. "The ideal sports official is a saint . . . no one but a saint could exhibit all of the psychological traits necessary to be a competent referee or um-

48

pire." These personality characteristics include tolerance, humility, self-confidence, ojectivity, and an ability to make quick, decisive decisions under fire.

"If officiating is so demanding, why then do people do it?" Dr. Roy Askins, a professor of social psychology who officiates part-time, has discovered several reasons. The most common motivation for pursuing the interest was earning extra money, remaining close to athletics in some capacity, and enjoying a position of some status and power.

REFEREE magazine, the only publication dedicated to officials, has a list of guidelines that you should ask yourself before getting started:

- Am I competitive and hard driven enough?
- Am I in control under pressure?
- Do I like to be a "tough guy" with an "I'll show you" type attitude?
- Do I consider myself confident, or do I come off cocky and arrogant in my presentation to others?
- Does crowd reaction affect me and do I hear everything said by having "rabbit ears?"
- Do I think before I act or speak?

The above questions are merely rhetoric of the situations you will be faced with. If you're not sure on how you may react to intense situations, there's no better way to find out than to simply go out and "do it."

Getting Started

To get a taste of the officiating scene, call upon a local recreation center, an adult intramural program, or any school sponsored league who are in dire need of officials. You may pick up a rule book and basic equipment for a minimal cost at a sporting goods store and attend referees' clinics that are sponsored by municipal athletic departments.

There is always a shortage of referees for lower levels and while the pay won't get you rich, it will provide valuable experience in addition to giving you a better understanding of the game you are partaking.

Remember though, there is no substitute for knowledge of the rules at any level of competition. Also by dressing the part and presenting a firm yet tolerable disposition, you will ward off a majority of the problems that you may have encountered early during the contest by gaining the respect of the players.

Once you become seriously interested in this profession, it is highly recommended to consider membership in a local officials' association as well as contacting your state's high school athletic league to become certified (if necessary).

Officiating also provides excellent part-time employment for the sports oriented student who has the necessary flexible schedule to officiate during the afternoon hours. As novice officials improve their level of competency, they will have the opportunity to take upon higher caliber games which may lead to a major tournament or championship event.

Even though there never seems to be enough qualified officials, nevertheless the upward movement to the collegiate ranks involves a very stringent process. Officials must have worked numerous tournaments to be considered for Division II & III competition. It is during these events that they are critiqued and receive recommendations from coaches and conferences for possible future upward mobility.

The next step involves applying to major Division I conferences which will have their own individual criteria and requirements for acceptance. An official should be careful not to wait too long in his career to make this move otherwise he may become stagnant in one level of play and never be given another consideration.

College officials receive very good per game stipends including travel expenses for out-of-town contests. Most businessmen enjoy college officiating better because it has the greater share of its schedules on evenings and weekends.

Opportunities are abundant in all areas of officiating especially within female sports and athletic activities that are less publicized. With the rapid growth in soccer, referees in this sport can practically pick their own schedules, while club sports that utilize judges such as gymnastics and figure skating, also are in demand of qualified officials and will thus handsomely compensate the people for their services.

Salaries vary widely among sports, but most high school varsity contests will pay $30-$40 per event. Small college games usually will have stipends ranging from $50-$100 per game plus traveling expenses.

On the professional front, an experienced official in the NHL or NBA can earn a figure of $55,000 annually as compared to an average salary of $40,000 for baseball umpires. For those who think they would enjoy the part-time career of an NFL referee, these men in stripes earn $500 for each Sunday afternoon tilt and up to $3,000 for the Super Bowl!

Officiating Schools

Although a study of readership of REFEREE magazine indicates that most officials enter the profession as a side income and will become proficient by attending local clinics, future officials will receive more sophisticated developmental instruction through formal officiating schools. This form of training will also provide additional credibility when applying to various conferences.

Listed below are camps and schools that provide specialized instruction in becoming a seasoned official:

Wendelstedt Umpire School

Harry Wendelstedt, who has worked in World Series, All Star, and Championship Playoff competition, is regarded by baseball people as one of the game's most competent officials. The school's specific purpose . . . "is to provide supervised training for young people to quality for umpire positions in professional, college or amateur baseball." Class sessions run for five weeks from January to February. Even though no jobs are promised, some exceptional students do receive appointments right after completion of the program while others may be called upon at a later date.

Interested persons should contact:

Harry Wendelstedt, Jr.
88 South Street Andrews Drive
Armond Beach, FL 32074

(904) 872-4879

Nationwide Basketball Referees Camp

Each summer in Indiana, Maryland, and Georgia, clinician Charlie Bloodworth sponsors a 4-day camp that attracts aspiring and active basketball referees from around the country. All phases of officiating from mechanics to personality development are emphasized. Each ref will be given the opportunity to work with and be critiqued by nationally known NCAA officials Hank Nichols and Dan Shea as well as a staff of referees who have participated in the most recent NCAA tournament.

If you wish additional information on this highly touted camp, contact:

Nationwide Referee Camp
3694 Rex Road
Rex, Georgia 30273

(404) 876-5541

Joe Brinkman Umpire School

This famed American League umpire holds two 5 week sessions yearly — (1) in California, and (1) in Florida at the previous home of the Houston Astros. With the use of video equipment lead instructors John McSherry (N.L.) and Nick Brenigan (A.L.) will personally teach you every aspect of umpiring necessary to make it in the professional circuit.

Interested persons should contact:

Joe Brinkman Umpire School
1021 Indian River Drive
Cocoa, FL 32922

(305) 639-1515

Blue Chip Officials Camp

Each year Mr. Ed Trexler is invited to put on his 3-day clinic at numerous sites throughout the country in football, basketball, and softball. This traveling camp has recently returned from Germany and the Far East and is expected to offer a full slate each summer.

If you would like to schedule a camp in your area or wish to attend the nearest sponsored clinic, contact:

Mr. Ed Trexler, Director
Blue Chip Officials Camp
2076 Mirton Drive
Tempe, AZ 85282

(602) 965-3526

Mickey Owen Umpire School
The site of America's internationally recognized baseball camp is also the home of an established umpire school. The school, which runs from May to July in 1 or 2 week segments, is operated in a cooperative effort with the National Baseball Congress' National Association of Umpires. Both novice and seasoned umpires from the ages of 15-50 have attended the school headed by former pro umpire Carl Lewton. The basic format includes rules study, mechanics instruction, and considerable field experience.

For a free packet of information, contact:

Mickey Owen Umpire School
Dept. NS-85
Miller, Missouri 65707

(417) 452-3111

Baksetball Officials' Opportunities

The 800 officiating program which is under the direction of Bob Murrey, represents more than just a basketball camp. This unique camp offers its participants opportunities in coinciding vacations with learning seminars, optional investment plans, leads for job placement, and the flexibility of choosing sites and dates convenient to the basketball official. 800 has been organized at the request of officials throughout the United States who have expressed a desire to improve themselves as referees, regardless of their level of experience. Every official will attend lectures, officiate a minimum of twice a day, and spend time learning from Division I instructors in one-on-one situations.

To learn more about the 800 program, contact:

800
512 S. Hanley
S-92
Clayton, MO 63105

(314) 725-3843

If you cannot take the time to attend a formal program or simply want to enjoy your involvement more as a hobby, one of the best ways to stay on top of officiating is to subscribe to REFEREE magazine. This monthly publication contains updates, current issues, profiles of successful officials, and tips for improvement.

For information on obtaining a subscription, write:

REFEREE
P.O. Box 161
Frankville, WI 53126

(414) 632-8855

Doing it

While gaining experience, attempt to master the rules of your sport keeping abreast of recent changes, interpretations, and emphases. This technical knowledge is important, but so is the development of your personality traits as an official. Continully self-critique your performances.

When you feel you are ready to make a move to the collegiate ranks or professional minor leagues, write to the administrative office of the league in which you might like to officiate and ask about the criteria they require. Each conference has an assigning secretary and you may obtain the address in the directory section of this book. A couple of special addresses are as follows:

Office for Baseball Umpire Development
P.O. Box A
225 Fourth Street South

Amateur Softball Association
2801 N.E. 50th
Oklahoma City, OK 73111
(404) 424-5266

As a final thought, despite the criticism officials receive there exists a quiet admiration for the role they provide. Al McGuire, former Marquette University basketball coach, sums it up best. "Nobody, but nobody, got on officials more than I. . . . Conversely, no one has more respect for these dedicated people and the difficult, thankless job that they do so well."

Strength & Conditioning Coaches

This is fast becoming a vital position in both the professional and amateur circles. Today's athletes are not only required to cooperate in off-season programs for increased performance, but it also has been proven that weight and agility training, as well as other forms of conditioning, can serve as a preventive force to certain types of injuries. As a return benefit to the athlete, this increased attention to bodily functions may also prolong the playing longevity of his/her career.

Strength coaches in the past served as both a part-time exercise specialist and as a team coach, but now they are hired in full-time capacities with no additional duties. These fitness specialists may be required to serve as a psychologist of sorts since the ability to motivate athletes is vital to success of any rehabilitative or strength program. When working with an injured athlete, strength coaches will work in conjunction with possibly a physical therapist, a trainer, or a doctor.

A strong background in anatomy and exercise physiology along with personal lifting expertise are necessary requirements to enter this field. There is current movement to require strength coaches to become a member of the National Strength Coaches Organization as a means to set up its own certification program.

Professional consultants are paid handsomely for their services, but due to the budding nature of this career, many collegiate strength coaches are compensated from only $14,000 to $18,000 annually.

Groundskeepers

With the onset of artificial surfaces, the landscaping artists of yesteryear are fast becoming a dying breed. Yet if you talk to any professional athlete who competes on natural grass, they'll be quick to tell you, especially around playoff time in football, which fields and groundskeepers have the best reputations.

Many state-run universities offer courses in agronomy — the science of grass and soil management — which can prepare students for numerous occupations requiring this knowledge. A person need not have a degree in agronomy to become a groundskeeper, but advancement is not as easily attainable without one.

It is not uncommon for a major golf course to pay its head groundskeeper $40,000 to $50,000 annually. On the other hand, groundskeeper at a major university or with a major league stadium generally will not receive more than $25,000 yearly. The importance of these imaginative people is best illustrated by professional football franchises who may have to share a facility with several other sports tenants or compete in an unpredictable climate. Upon completion of a successful season, teams have been known to share their respect for the groundskeeper by often sharing their playoff monies with him. This practice has rarely been done with any other non-team member.

Equipment Managers

At times this can be a thankless position (as many of you ex-high school and college managers know), but this occupation does allow for the sports enthusiast to display much expertise and creativity without any long, involved training. These support staff members at the college and professional levels are required at times during peak seasons to perform around the clock.

An equipment manager must know his equipment, its styles, and its safety measures. He must also keep in tune with the latest technology and latest market lines. And when a piece of equipment does not meet the needs or body configuration of an athlete due to injury or comfort, the equipment specialist will become an improvisor able to modify equipment without jeopardizing safety. It is at times like these that he may have to consult the trainer or manufacturer. In a sense, this person needs to be a part-time counselor understanding the players, their needs, their whims, and their frustrations. Many times the improvisation of the equipment will give the athlete a sense of added confidence (possibly a placebo effect) knowing that the adjustment may have made him a half-step faster.

There is no way to prepare for this job, no courses of study, and no degrees to obtain. It's more or less an education of on-the-job training. For the college student, it provides an excellent means of supplemental income or for receiving a scholarship.

Equipment people must be reliable, punctual, and quick thinkers considering that by missing even one play, a player's absence could cost the outcome of a game.

There are many job opportunities with a wide open market existing for women. Those at the college level can expect salaries in the $12,000-$18,000 range, while professional equipment personnel will receive wages from $18,000 to $22,000 with many receiving bonuses beyond their basic rates.

For further information, contact:

The Equipment Managers Association
Bowling Green State University
Bowling Green, OH 43402

Cinematographers

The use of movie film and video recording has risen in all sports over the last decade. No longer are football coaches the only ones who may benefit from this training aid, but other skill oriented activities have come to realize the advantages for performance analysis, teaching, scouting, and even in injury prevention.

Almost every professional organization hires cinematographers to cover their games and on occasion, their practices. The typical cinematographer will double as both a lab technician and a film librarian.

Becoming an assistant to an established cinematographer is one means of getting started. Experience is a vital factor here and may be the only aspect evaluated when you solicit contracts. This technologically skilled area presents benefits to a team that can't be accomplished within their organization.

With the emergence of videos and the popularity of the NFL films series and team hi-lites, opportunities will arise for the individual with innovative talent.

Performance Trainers

The most noted forms of trainers are those that work with horses in the racing scene and those who perform a multitude of duties with boxers.

Horse Trainers: The majority of horse trainers have a veterinarian background, and much like the human exercise physiologist, trainers will be well versed on nutrition, biomechanics and anatomical functions. Horse trainers are well compensated for, but their hours are long and all-consuming.

To enter this field, one must have a sincere interest in the well being of the animal population and be willing to be committed to continually keeping abreast with veterinary advancements. Opportunities will be more abundant in states where paramutual betting is legal. However, be ready to start from the ground floor up which may result in some very undesirable duties.

Boxing Trainers: The recent rebirth of boxing's popularity has allowed for the opening of gyms across the country. The boxing trainer acts as a manager-coach for the boxer preparing his or her protege in the technique of the sport and scheduling fight cards.

The more proficient trainer will have a knowledge of exercise principles, athletic training, film analysis, and expertise in dealing with the media. But before you get any grandiose ideas of being in the next Rocky movie, visit a local gym to see if you could be of any assistance. A boxing background would be most helpful if for nothing else, credibility's sake.

Keep in mind that few trainers make a living in this career, in fact most will do this as a hobby rather than as a steady job.

Additional Related Sports Fields

Health Clubs & Resorts

With the "thin is in" motto of the 80s, health and fitness centers are springing up in every neighborhood across the country. Though working for a health facility, tennis resort, or golf club may appear glamorous, the hours are long and the pay is minimal. Wages and profits are characteristically low due to the tremendous overhead that is created by providing varied fitness services. The only staff members earning a substantial living in this field are the instructing pros or the general managers.

Health management duties include staffing of personnel, scheduling of activities and events, solicitation of members, and continuous budget examination. For those who enjoy a fitness environment and don't mind a slow but steady climb to higher management, there is room for growth in the health maintenance industry.

Opportunities in this field are numerous but in order to make any considerable movements within a club, a degree in business administration with possible coursework in physical education is essential. Salaries in the mid-teens are to be expected with increases and bonuses few and far between.

An organization worth noting is as follows:

Club Managers Association of America
7615 Winterberry Place
Bethesda, MD 20817

(301) 229-3600

Industrial Recreation

With an emphasis on health and fitness, the rising costs of insurance premiums, and the addition of financial losses due to absenteeism and injury compensation, corporations are beginning to develop "in-house" wellness programs in an attempt to create a healthier workforce. Positions in this slowly developing concept are ideal for the sports-minded individual who has a flair for corporate managerial skills. Depanding on the philosophy of the firm, typical functions may include scheduling sports leagues, designing a fitness facility, developing fitness programs, and managing after-hours special interest club functions.

Educational requirements include a bachelor's degree with courses in personnel, budgeting, finance, recreation, and possibly physical education. Opportunities are somewhat scarce but the trend will be for more corporations to have complete service programs by the 1990s. Most positions are currently filled from within the management ranks or from those who organized and maintained current programs on a volunteer basis. A salary for a program director in a major corporation could exceed the mid-$30,000's.

For more information on organizations, education and employment opportunities, write:

National Employee Services & Recreation Association
20 North Wacker, Suite 2020
Chicago, IL 60606

National Recreation & Park Association
3101 Park Center Drive
Alexandria, VA 22209

American Association of Fitness
Directors in Business and Industry
700 Anderson Hill Road
Purchase, NY 10577

(914) 253-2473

56

CHAPTER 7

EDUCATION

Within the realm of sports education, there are two distinct career routes you could pursue. One is in a teaching capacity working within the educational system. The other is that of a practitioner in the application of sports sciences principles. Each branch of sports education interrelates with the other: skill training serves as a practical laboratory for academic studies while academic studies on the other hand become a source of new ideas and techniques for coaches and instructors.

To be proficient at the sports sciences, a marriage must exist between the intellectual and experiential components of athletics. If an individual enters sports from an exact discipline (i.e. sociology or psychology), then he/she will need to increase his/her expertise in physical education applications and sports knowledge. At the same time, those already experienced as athletes and coaches may need to take a step back to understand the intellectual and theoretical aspects of their training.

However this interrelationship between theory and research with the practical application approach has not transpired well in the United States. This lack of awareness, coupled with the public's apprehension to utilize the many sports sciences advancements, has created little demand for the practicing sports consultants. The result of this present state is that a majority of those employed in these fields will remain in an educational environment performing research with any private consultation relegated to that of a part-time avocation.

Physical Education

Physical educators are involved in teaching and developing "the art and science of human movement." Despite the emphasis placed upon physical fitness in the schools in the last decade, test scores of today's youth are actually decreasing in their state of physical conditioning. The current physical state of young students represents the biggest challenge confronting physical educators in the 80s.

A majority of those working in physical education are employed by the school system, but with budget cuts and diminishing student populations, the trend will be to seek career opportunities in the private sector at resorts, clubs, and social agencies. There are other "sidelines" that P.E. personnel with their flexible schedules are able to take advantage of. As mentioned earlier, some will take upon coaching duties, officiating, aerobic instruction, or consulting in fitness design.

Even though a physical education career may appear ever changing, there is little room for upward mobility unless a master's degree is attained. Many choose to take additional coursework in administration or use their graduate work to secure a collegiate teaching position.

Physical education can be divided into several factions: elementary education, secondary instruction, and college teaching. The age group preference is strictly a personal one, but keep in mind that many students will be in your class as a requirement, not as an elective. Being able to motivate young people to commit themselves to self-improvement may take precedence over other aspects of teaching physical education.

The main responsibility for a physical education instructor at any level is to develop a wide variety of skills in students such as: agility, balance, coordination, endurance, flexibility, power, rhythm, strength, timing, and other psychomotor abilities.

When choosing a college for educational training, it is important to make sure that it is accredited for the purposes of acquiring a teaching license. Check with your state requirements when developing your curriculum.

The outlook for teaching physical educators remains only fair. Therefore it becomes imperative to diversify your education and experience in order to take advantage of opportunities that may arise in a non-P.E. environment.

An undergraduate degree will provide earnings from $12,500 to $27,000 for a 10 month appointment commensurate with educational and practical experience. For those with master's degrees, the scale and possible opportunities increases immensely.

Two noted physical education associations that may lend assistance in choosing a school or securing employment are as follows:

AAHPERD
(American Alliance for Health, Physical Education, Recreation & Dance)
1900 Association Drive
Reston, Virginia 22091

AAPEHR
(American Association for Physical Education, Health & Recreation)
1201 16th Street N.W.
Washington, D.C. 20036

Sports Psychology

An emerging field of study that has recently created considerable interest is that of developing the mental side of athletic performance. Whether the issue is mental toughness, getting psyched, coping with pressure, or maintaining concentration, athletes are constantly seeking techniques that may provide the "competitive edge."

Though a relatively new concept in the development of American athletes, sports psychology has made its only inroads in the amateur circles and has yet to be accepted in the professional ranks. Without an established market, sports psychologists continue to struggle for recognition as most practitioners have clients in other walks of life or merely remain teaching professors at the collegiate level.

Sports psychology should not be confused with hypnotism, even though such altered relaxed states are utilized in the processes for visualization of a performance skill, mental rehearsal before a competition, or during biofeedback training. Batteries of interpersonal inventories are common tools facilitated by sports psychologists in assessing personality traits that may affect performance.

Sports consultants have recently begun to take active roles in working with athletes who suffer from alcohol and drub abuse in addition to serving as instructors for youth coaching effectiveness and certification programs. There is much concern with the direction which youth sports is taking especially in its character formation processes. It is the hope that sports psychology can address such issues and scientifically educate coaches on the "hows" and "whys" in motor learning and child development.

Other conditions that may require the expertise of a sports psychologist are seen in cases of burnout, anorexia and bulemia, aggressive behavior, injury rehabilitation, and post-career life transitions for professional athletes.

A current controversy exists with the future legal status of sports psychology. Since a majority of these specialized consultants have completed their educational training in either a physical education or motor learning program, licensed psychologists question the validity of their psychological counseling background. It will be some time before this issue will be resolved but the following organizations have been found to further the advancement of sports psychology:

AAASP (Association for the Advancement of Applied Sport Psychology)

The purpose of this recently created organization is to promote the development of psychological theory, research, and intervention strategies in sport psychology. The organizers of the AAASP believed there was a strong need to insure that sport psychology is recognized as an orderly body of professional researchers and practitioners applying scientific principles in a systematic manner.

For further information on membership to this dynamic group, contact:

Charles J. Hardy
Dept. of Physical Education
University of North Carolina
Chapel Hill, NC 27514

NASPSPA (North American Society for Psychology of Sport & Physical Activity)

The NASPSPA functions to encourage the study of human behavior in sport and physical activity and to improve the quality of teaching and research in sport psychology, motor development, and motor learning. The society's members include scholars from a variety of behavioral sciences and professions.

To learn more about the society, write:

Dr. Deborah Feltz
Youth Sport Institute
Room 210, IM Sport Circle
Michigan State University
East Lansing, MI 48824

Other sports psychology special interest groups include:

Academy for the Psychology of Sports
2062 Arlington Avenue
Toledo, OH 43609

(419) 385-4357

Philosophical Society for the Study of Sport
Dr. James Genasci
Springfield College
Dept. of Health & Physical Education
Springfield, MA 01101

Education

There is an increasing number of graduate programs in sports psychology now being offered. Consult the following list of institutions to determine if their curriculum meets both your educational and career goals since some will be more research based while others will be more application oriented.

Department of Physical Education
University of Alberta
Edmonton, Alberta, Canada T6G 249
(403) 432-2128

Department of Physical Education
University of Arizona
Tucson, AZ 85721
(607) 621-6989

Department of Physical Education
Arizona State University
Tempe, AZ 85287
(602) 965-7664

Department of Physical Education
University of California, Berkeley
Berkeley, CA 94720
(415) 865-3179

Los Angeles, CA 90024
(213) 825-4210

New York, NY 10027
(212) 678-3323

Tallahassee, FL 32306
(904) 644-2829

Champaign, IL 61801
(217) 333-6487

Iowa City, IA 52242
(319) 353-3532

Baton Rouge, LA 70803
(504) 388-2036

Amherst, MA 01002
(413) 545-0621

East Lansing, MI 48824-1034
(517) 355-1824

Montreal, Quebec, Canada H3C 3J7
(514) 343-7784

Denton, TX 76203
(817) 565-3430

Penn State University
University Park, PA 16802
(814) 863-0540

University of Ottawa
Ottawa, Ontario K1N 6N5
(613) 564-5946

Waterloo, Ontario, Canada NZL 3G1

Madison, WI 53706
(608) 262-2457

Orinda, CA 94563
(415) 254-0110

San Diego, CA 92182
(619) 693-4720

To receive a comprehensive directory of graduate programs in applied sport psychology which will also feature bids on each institution's program, contact:

Michael L. Sachs, Ph.D.
P.O. Box 4005
Timonium, MD 21093

Exercise Physiology

The movment towards maximizing athletic performance has expanded to the application of exercise physiology principles. The study of exercise physiology involves the analysis and improvement of cardiopulmonary endurance and capacity, muscle power, and joint flexibility.

Like other emerging sports sciences, exercise physiology practitioners have yet to gain the respect they deserve int he private sector of health. Therefore the greater proportion of exercise physiologists are involved with research at human performance laboratories usually at university fitness centers. But for those who are able to be employed in a consulting capacity, they will more than likely serve in evaluating the potential of athletes, developing conditioning and injury prevention programs for teams in conjunction with coaches and other sports medicine personnel, and assisting elite and weekend athletes to achieve fitness.

Exercise physiologists utilize "state of the art" technology in evaluating performance and implementing training techniques. The combination of slow motion films, videotapes, and computer analysis provide direction in perfecting performance.

At the present time, the field remains wide open for the research oriented individual but somewhat restricted for those seeking employment in the private sector. Exercise physiologists who are able to secure a corporate fitness directorship can earn upwards of $35,000 to $90,000 at a national health center. Teaching and research counterparts can expect a beginning salary in the low $20,000's.

Exercise physiologists are one of the few sports sciences that requires its graduates to pass a national certification exam. There are some practitioners that have acquired only a master's degree, but the trend is to complete the doctoral program. Over half of the states in the union have at least one institution that offers an exercise physiology curriculum. When contacting the school of your choice for inquiry, address all materials through the Department of Physical Education.

Biomechanics

This science is a sister to the field of exercise physiology. Biomechanics involves the analysis and correction of athletic movement in relation to the body's musculoskeletal system. Employees that may best use these services include manufacturers of athletic equipment, research health centers, and fitness clubs. Since biomechanical testing is not in demand for individual consultation, job opportunities are limited. In addition to teaching and performing research at human performance laboratories, the best possibility for a practitioner position will be in corporate fitness applications.

Like exercise physiology, a master's degree leading to a doctorate will be required of interested students, but one drawback will be experienced in the salary structure which will not exceed the range of $17,000 to $35,000 annually.

Sports Sociology

Though a relatively unknown segment of the sports sciences, sports sociology involves the research and instruction of sports as social institution, social process, and structural social activity. The applications of this science are few and far between as most sports sociologists will be committed to research, writing and lecturing on the subject.

Since there has been little demand for the application of sports sociology, few institutions offer a structural program per se, but many do offer select courses in this area. A master's degree to doctorate in physical education with emphasis in sociology or a sociology degree with a concentration in physical education are necessary educational requirements. As in all academic careers, advancement comes through completing and publishing research as well as through teaching expertise.

The job market outlook is not encouraging and for those sports sociologists who can be innovative and aggressive, an earnings estimate would be in the range of $18,000 to $35,000 annually.

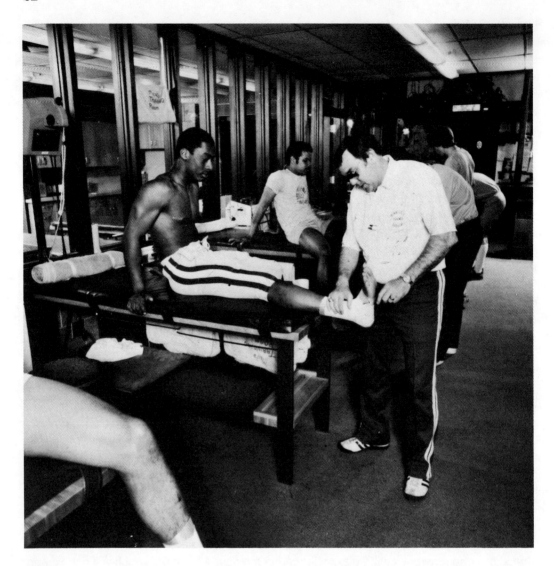

CHAPTER 8

SPORTS MEDICINE

America's infatuation with sports, which has led us to be a nation of fans, has taken upon a new direction in the 80s. The typical sports enthusiast's involvement once relegated to that of a passive spectator has now transcended to the role of an active participant. Today's "get involved" attitude is clearly evident upon examination of a recent study which indicates that 44% of the American population is participating in some form of athletic activity or fitness program. There is, however, one overriding side effect that has transpired through this fitness boom. That being an outgrowth of activity-related injuries. The drastic rise in the numerous physical disablements can usually be attributed to one of the following conditions: improper training techniques; poor levels of physical conditioning; or ignorance to the physical complexities of the activity.

Beginning fitness and recreational buffs are not the only ones experiencing an increase in injuries. With the increasing popularity of the numerous non-traditional sports cropping up almost daily, along with the exorbitant number of athletes starting to compete in the more established activities, the figure for those individuals having the potential to seek sports medicine assistance at one time or another is nearly exhaustive. In one year alone, the Department of Health, Education, and Welfare estimated that over one million sports related injuries occurred at the varsity level in high school and college sports. Taking into account players at all levels of play, from school age to the professional ranks, the following injury statistics were reported during a 12 month period of time:

Football   - 1,000,000
Basketball -   800,000
Baseball   -   500,000
Other   -   700,000

Another grim statistic revealed that during the '70s close to 200 disablements led to an athlete becoming a quadraplegic while an additional 100 injuries resulted in the death of a participant.

The onset of these sometimes uncommon injuries are often out of the ordinary everyday practices for most family physicians. Many may even require extensive rehabilitation for a full recovery which, once again, the general practitioner may not be equipped to attend. The emergence of athletic injuries has thus opened the door and created an imminent need for specially trained physicians and therapists.

It becomes apparent the impact sports medicine research has provided in the rehabilitative process, but of equal importance that has not received as much attention is the field's contributions to the prevention and diagnosing of potential injuries before they occur. Yet still another positive breakthrough that has evolved from sports medicine's advanced technology is in its physiological testing of new approaches to training techniques which can assist athletes in optimizing their levels of performance.

It should be noted that sports medicine's rehabilitative process does not include medical personnel alone, but also utilizes the expertise in a host of other interrelated specialties such as nutrition, kinesiology, exercise physiology, psychology, physical therapy, and even podiatry. Of all the sports associated careers that have been outlined in this publication, none will offer in the next decade a wider range of opportunities, provide for continued advancement and job security, or compensate its workforce as well than those positions in the sports medicine field.

The training involved in these highly specialized disciplines is both rigorous and very competitive, but due to a shortage of qualified practitioners in several areas, there should be an abundance of possible options for the patient and dedicated male or female. With an evolving interest in sports and a fitness-conscious society, the need for sports medicine services will continue to grow. The field will employ and attract all types of individuals from the person who is research minded to the scholar who desires to be application oriented.

Sports Physicians

In days gone by before the term sports medicine really had any legitimate meaning, a team doctor treated everything from broken bones to head colds. Sports specialization, an inevitable necessity seen in the numerous aforementioned careers, has now become a need in the ranks of medical doctors as well. The three distinct groups that comprise the physician specialist are as follows: Doctors of Medicine (M.D.); Doctors of Osteopathy (D.O.); and Doctors of Chiropractic (D.C.)

A good many M.D.'s offering services in sports medicine will be general practitioners (G.P.'s) serving as team physicians, while the majority of sports physicians involved in clinics and rehab centers will ultimately have their training as orthopedists. The orthopedist will be the primary caretaker of injured individuals authorized to make delicate decisions and, when necessary, supervise the follow-up treatment administered by other support personnel.

Osteopaths and chiropractors on the other hand have only begun to gain respect within the medical community and general public. Their roles as consultants to schools, teams, and health centers has now diverged into private practices since their patients are now able to utilize their health insurance coverage for their services.

To be proficient and credible as a sports physician, doctors must be trained in all procedures for the prevention, recognition, and treatment of soft tissue and skeletal injuries. Physicians should have a clear understanding of the sport in which they are involved including the mechanism of the injuries occurring, the protective gear and equipment utilized, and the emotional well being of its peformers with careful consideration of the especially young player.

The physician who undertakes the responsibility of being a team doctor must remain objective and firm with both coaches and parents when making a decision as to whether or not an injured player may be allowed to return to competition. The ethical considerations in these situations represents the one aspect that so many sports medicine doctors find most difficult to handle, especially when taking into account the emphasis placed on winning at all costs. There are many instances in which a physician will be forced to take action contrary to both the coach's or injured athlete's beliefs in as far as the player's ability to play incapacitated. It is times such as these that sports medicine personnel must maintain a sense of professional objectivity.

There are, unfortunately, universities and professional franchises that do employ therapists and doctors who are unethical and will thus perform any service or treatment to an injured athlete on direct orders from higher management. Such malpractices have left numerous athletes with permanent damage to their bodies or have had their careers shortened as a result of an incorrect diagnosis, by taking excessive dosages of pain killers, or by receiving improper rehabilitation treatment.

There is no place for unethical individuals in sports, much less in the medical profession. By being involved in any of the above malpractices, you will not only risk your professional career, but also the credibility of the sports medicine field.

Orthopedists

As has already been indicated, a greater percentage of all sports physicians will have an orthopedic background. Orthopedists, who are also surgeons, will treat injuries and abnormalities of the skeletal system and musculature by implementing a wide range of techniques to restore the athlete to his/her playing capacities.

Few orthopedists will restrict their practice to sports injuries alone and therefore will usually be a staff member at a hospital or a rehabilitative clinic. Long work days are the norm, but these specialists will in return enjoy fine working conditions and a position of prestige in the medical community. Orthopedists earn excellent salaries with yearly incomes in the area of $100,000.

The outlook for these physicians is excellent for both men and women, but the competition for entrance into medical school will always remain fierce.

Education

Despite the demand for its services and a growing interest in careers within the sports medicine field, there remains no formal educational programs leading to a recognized sports medicine degree. The only route at this time is to attend one of the 126 accredited medical schools in the United States.

Upon completion of a 4 year undergraduate degree and acceptance into a medical school, those interested in sports medicine will most likely pursue an orthopedic residency lasting from 2-5 years.

There are, however, numerous institutions that offer specialty course offerings in selected areas of sports medicine. Also, a group of physicians have now organized the Sports Medicine Curriculum Study Group in order to identify which subjects need to be taught to cultivate competencies in this area.

Further information concerning sports medical doctors may be obtained from the following:

American Medical Association
535 N. Dearborn Street
Chicago, IL 60610

Association of American Medical Colleges
The DuPont Circle N.S. Suite 200
Washington, D.C. 20036

American Orthopoedic Society for Sports Medicine
70 West Hubbard Street, Suite 202
Chicago, IL 60610

The following publications would offer excellent reading material on trends and issues in sports medicine:

Medicine & Science in Sports and Exercise
1440 Monroe Street
Madison, WI 53706

(608) 262-3632

The Physician in Sports & Medicine
McGraw Hill Book Company
4530 West 77th Street
Minneapolis, MN 55435

(612) 835-3222

Doctor of Osteopathy

Like the orthopedists, D.O.'s will concern themselves with the muscular-skeletal system of the body — bones, muscles, ligaments, and nerves. Osteopaths, however, offer their patients an additional service of health care — manipulation. The use of hands in manipulative therapy is the basic treatment of osteopathy.

Osteopathy places its emphasis on treating the "whole person." Those specializing in osteopathy would therefore take into consideration the total health of a person when treating an injury.

Osteopaths, like chiropractors, have fought a long battle to gain the respect of the medical profession. By not gaining total acceptance as a healer, the average salary will therefore be lower than that of an M.D., probably $40,000 annually.

Their educational training is similar to that of a medical doctor with the addition of osteopathic manipulation. Osteopaths must also undertake residencies upon graduation which will eventually lead to licensing necessary to practice.

For those interested in an emerging sports medicine career that offers an excellent working environment, additional information may be obtained by contacting:

American Association of Osteopath Medicine
4720 Montgomery Lane
Washington, D.C. 20014

American Osteopathic Association
212 East Ohio Street
Chicago, IL 60611

Doctor of Chiropractic

Chiropractic doctors implement manipulation (adjustments) as their primary treatment. It is their belief that a person's health is directly related to the nervous system. It is theorized that any interference with the nervous system will impair the body's normal functions which will in return lower resistance to disease. Therefore, D.C.'s will place the emphasis of their treatment with the spinal column to restore proper functioning.

Chiropractors do not believe in prescription drugs or surgery, but as a supplement to their manipulation techniques, they will utilize water, acupuncture, massage, ultrasound and various temperature controlled therapy modalities. Special diets, nutritional supplements, and exercise are commonly prescribed during rehabilitation by D.C.'s.

The "cold war" that once existed between the American Medical Association and chiropractic medicine has dramatically rescinded in recent years. In fact, both disciplines have learned to understand the importance of both practices to the point where each will refer patients to their counterparts if it is in the best interest of the injured athlete.

With the recent approval of chiropractic services now a part of health insurance coverage, the popularity of chiropractic approaches to holistic health will continue to grow and receive acceptance. Holistic medicine's emphasis on prevention represents the philosophical trend to health care of the future.

Education

Though few people realize it, the educational training of chiropractors is as intense if not more so in selected subjects than those physicians who attend the more traditional medical schools.

Upon completion of their educational requirements and clinical experience, D.C.'s must pass the licensing requirements in the state in which they wish to practice. For those wishing to perform as a sports medicine practitioner, there is a certification program which requires additional coursework and the completion of an application examination.

As the field develops, so will the earnings. Chiropractors currently average from $40,000 to $50,000 annually in an established clinic.

One of the most well known institutions for formalized chiropractic training is the Northwestern College of Chiropractic Medicine located in Minneapolis, Minnesota. A unique feature of the school is its sports medicine certification curriculum. For more information on admission requirements, contact:

Dr. Trzeslawski
Northwestern College of Chiropractic
2501 West 84th Street
Bloomington, MN 55431

(612) 888-4777

Organizations that may provide additional insight into this prospering career are as follows:

Council on Sports Injuries
American Chiropractic Association
2200 Grand Avenue
Des Moines, IA 50312

Council on Chiropractic Education
3209 Ingersoll Avenue
Des Moines, IA 50312

International Chiropractors Association
1901 L Street
M.S. Suite 800
Washington, D.C. 20036

Physical Therapy
Physical therapists are involved with patients who have become disabled from an accident, a birth defect, an illness, or possibly an injury during sports participation. A good share of sports therapist's time will be spent with athletes referred by a physician for prescribed rehabilitation

following surgery or recovery from a disabling sports injury. It is at this point that the main function of a physical therapist is to administer therapy in order to restore function, relieve pain, prevent reinjury and return the athlete to action as soon as possible.

Rehabilitation treatments include: exercise for increasing strength, endurance, and range of motion; application of temperature controlled modalities; ultrasound; acupuncture to relieve pain; or massage techniques. The type or combination of treatments that will be employed will vary upon the nature of the injury or recovery period.

In addition to healing skills, physical therapists will need to have good interpersonal abilities. Besides working closely with patients they will be required to communicate effectively with numerous health care personnel from radiologists to orthopedists.

Most sports physical therapists will become certified as athletic trainers providing they meet the requirements for certification and have been recommended from an acting team physician or a NATA-certified trainer.

In looking at experience factors the sports therapist should be concerned with the training and care of injured athletes; the alteration of protective padding; a knowedge of nutrition and body maintenance skills; the development of conditioning programs; administering preseason screening examinations; the selection and fitting of equipment; and a keen awareness to the type of playing and environmental conditions in which the athletes will compete.

The outlook for physical therapists is excellent considering that there are far more job opportunities than applicants. Sports medicine though is only one of the many segments in which P.T.'s perform. The highest percentage of therapists will be employed by hospitals, clinics and research centers, spending a considerable amount of time working with the elderly.

The current shortage of rehabilitation specialists will allow for a continued increase in the salary scale which is the in the range of $15,000 to $40,000 annually.

Education

There are more than 90 colleges and universities in the United States that offer accredited undergraduate programs in the general field of physical therapy. However, by 1990, the American Physical Therapy Association has mandated that each certified member must have a Master's in physical therapy. Presently, those specializing in sports physical therapy are able to do so only at the graduate level anyway.

Aspiring students will take courses that are both theory and application based. Typical studies will be in pathology, pharmacology, therapeutic exercise, and athletic training courses emphasizing the evaluation and treatment of patients through nerve and muscle stimulation currents.

One of the more prominent sports medicine curriculums is offered at Ball State University in Muncie, Indiana. The focus of Ball State's curriculum is on turning out well rounded practitioners that are able to step in any sports medicine environment.

For a listing of accredited schools and additional information on this specialty that is in even greater demand than sports, contact:

American Physical Therapy Association
1156 15th Street, N.W.
Washington, D.C. 20005

(202) 466-2070

ATHLETIC TRAINING

Athletic trainers represent the core of all sports medicine practitioners. Their basic duties consist of the implementation of injury prevention programs, initiation of immediate treatment for an injured athlete, and the supervision of injury rehabilitation procedures set forth by the team physician. Undoubtedly a trainer's skill expertise must be varied considering that he/she will be required to attend to the simple treatment of cuts and abrasions to the imaginative custom-tailoring of protective equipment. Since athletic trainers work within the traditions of numerous sports, their roles could very well expand into the unique needs of each. Specialty functions may very well include establishing conditioning programs, planning menus, supervising diets, and even serving as a counselor of sports to the players themselves.

Though it may appear that the main function of athletic training is aimed to deal with injuries "after the fact," Otho Davis, NFL trainer and Executive Director of the National Athletic Trainers Association, believes, "The most important role of the trainer is to prevent an injury from occurring. At the professional level a player cannot afford to even miss practice." Otho also feels his greatest satisfaction "comes from seeing an individual return to maximum potential by performing well following an injury."

A proficient trainer will have a sense for the personalities of everyone with whom he or she must be associated. This is so because a trainer must identify who truly needs assistance and those who are either faking or are making more out of the injury. On the other hand it is necessary to know those individuals who will do anything or say anything to be able to play full-time once again. A common dilemma exists with freshman athletes, especially in football. Many are not accustomed to playing with everyday injury nuances and therefore must be made to understand the different types of pain. Even adjusting to the many carpet scrapes and burns from artificial surfaces requires an acclimation period.

Trainers must be careful not to be influenced by coaches or management who may want an athlete to return to playing status sooner than rehabilitation will allow. By being in the middle of such situations, a trainer will only then begin to realize the commitment he/she has vowed to adhere to in the ethical practices of the profession.

Before you contemplate entrance into this field, be absolutely certain that you have a sincere interest in athletics and even more importantly the well being of those involved in sport. Trainers are for the most part healers and must therefore be sensitive to the needs and concerns of each individual athlete. In addition to being "people oriented," other necessary attributes include an ability to work well with one's hands, a sense of ingenuity, meticulously clean health habits, and an understanding that the dedication to serve others will involve long, many times unusual hours.

Professional Athletic Teams

There exists much diversity among the working environments for athletic trainers from sport to sport and even within each organization. A major league football franchise may employ as many as four full-time trainers in addition to part-time trainers for game days, while a professional soccer team may only contract training services utilizing a sports clinic should an injury arise. Unmistakenly though, professional football is the ultimate goal and hotbed for every aspiring trainer.

Employment with a professional team is glamorous, exciting, and provides numerous additional benefits, but unfortunately securing such positions will continue to be a difficult task.

Collegiate Teams

The greatest number of potential opportunities exists for athletic trainers at major universities, four year colleges, and junior colleges. Though the working conditions may resemble any typical professional organization, the major difference will be that the trainer will work with numerous teams and sports through the course of a season. A major university will usually employ only a head athletic trainer with several asistants and student trainers. For students, the pay will be minimal but the experience that will be acquired will prove to be invaluable in both securing a position and in the treatment process.

Sports Medicine Clinics

With an emergence of specialized sports centers rapidly increasing in numbers across the country, the demand for certified trainers has increased drastically. The salary and working hours at such clinics and hospitals are surpassed only by those trainers employed in the professional ranks.

The one possible drawback that may exist here is that a majority of a trainer's time spent in this type of setting will be involved only in areas of treatment and rehabilitation of injured athletes and recreational enthusiasts. It is not uncommon for the dedicated therapist to become frustrated with the recreational athlete who may not be as disciplined in the rehabilitative process as the competitive athlete that he/she is accustomed to working with. Since a trainer in this situation may not always have the luxury to have a "feel" for the clientele to be served, that individual must learn to develop a sound judge of character. In any case, when choosing a perspective clinic for employment, find out who the general population is that seeks assistance and the role in which you will be required to perform beyond normal conditions. This may in the long run prevent any future job dissatisfaction.

Training

To secure a position as an athletic trainer, a sound educational and experiential background without a doubt will be necessary. There are many routes to pursue but many of today's practitioners started their careers as team managers or student trainers at their high school or college. For others their interest began by attending one of the many trainee camps and clinics that are continually being held throughout the country.

Even though there still exist states who do not require licensing to be employed as a trainer, there is an organization that was formed to certify trainers and lend credibility to the profession. This umbrella group called the National Athletic Trainers Association (NATA) was inaugurated with a goal to exchange concepts, ideas, and advancements in athletic training as well as promote interest in the prevention and care of athletic injuries. Probably the one single most contribution the NATA has made since its development is its established guidelines to accrediting institutions in meeting educational requirements for certification.

For those wishing to become involved in a more formalized training format, there are some 50 schools accredited by the NATA across the United States which will qualify recipients for the certification program. If you are already in school and would like to begin yuor educational preparation, the recommended courses to be taken at the high school level include first aid, health, biology, physics, and general science courses, while college bound students should pursue subjects in anatomy, physiology, kinesiology, nutrition, exercise, and school health.

NATA's standards for graduate level certification requires a bachelors degree from one of its accredited institutions, completion of advanced athletic training courses, and a minimum of 300 clock hours of clinical experience.

At the present time, there are four ways to become certified by the NATA:

1) Obtain a degree at one of the accredited athletic training curriculums.
2) Undertake an apprenticeship. This route is utilized when the educational requirements are met but have not been taken from an approved institution. Certification may therefore be attained by completion of the required courses, a letter of recommendation from an acting team physician or NATA trainer, and supervised NATA clinical experience of 1800 hours over a two year period of time.
3) Become a special consideration athletic trainer whereby certification is recommended for those active trainers not pursuing the prescribed NATA process.
4) Be certified as a physical therapist by meeting the general requirements and presenting letters of recommendation from an acting team physician and a NATA-certified trainer.

There is a current movement to establish licensing or some form of prescribed regulation for all states in the union. The NATA would also like to implement a series of oral, practical, and written exams for future licensing procedures. With this in mind, prospective trainers should plan accordingly when establishing their curricula and practical clinician programs.

The Future

The need for certified athletic trainers will only continue to increase in its demand as it is estimated that high schools alone offer the possibility of 10,000-20,000 jobs! Currently, women athletic trainers are in short supply as are trainers needed to cover the astronomical numbers of youth contests. While salaries remainonly moderate to good, $12,000-$30,000, potential salaries will increase in the years ahead.

For more information regarding accredited institutions, certification, or possible employment, contact:

National Athletic Trainers Association
P.O. Drawer 1865
Greenville, NC 27834

(919) 752-1725

Other organizations to contact concerning clinics, camps, or general knowledge, are as follows:

Cramer First Aid Products
Box 1001
Gardner, KS 66030

American Athletic Trainer's Association & Certification Board
638 West Duarte Road
Arcadia, CA 91006

(213) 445-1978

National Athletic Health Association
575 East Hardy Street
Inglewood, CA 90301

(213) 674-1600

Sports Nutrition

In the athlete's quest to gain the "competitive edge," the relationship between nutrition and performance has recently been discovered to be a key factor. The advances in sports nutrition and the acceptance by both the public and medical community of its importance in attaining total health and wellness will allow sports nutritionists to perform a major role in enhancing performances in the years ahead.

Most nutritionists involved in sports will serve in a consulting capacity, usually self-employed in a private practice. Their function will be mainly concerned with the the analysis and development of the athlete's diet for teams, sports medicine clinics and camps, offering expertise in weight control, pre-game meals, and vitamin-mineral supplementation.

A good number of practicing sports nutritionists have acquired their education and background in medicine or nutrition with their experience being gained many times as a nurse or dietician. Those wishing to pursue this growing field will need to complete at least a Master's in nutrition with a doctorate degree desirable for added credibility.

Nutritionists are receiving excellent fees for their services as earnings from $20,000 to $80,000 annually can be expected depending upon the type of private practice or position.

Podiatry

It is estimated that 80% of all people have foot problems in one form or another and realizing that nearly every sport puts a great strain on its participants' feet, the need for podiatric care becomes ever so important. These Doctors of Podiatric Medicine (D.P.M.) are concerned with the diagnosis, treatment, and prevention of foot and lower-extremity injuries. D.P.M.'s will utilize a variety of methods including medical, surgical, and physical techniques when attending to disablements and diseases.

Podiatrists may practice privately or be a part of a hopsital staff or sports clinic. D.P.M.'s will enjoy excellent working conditions and will not be required to work the many long hours as other fellow sports medicine practitioners.

Aspiring podiatrists must complete an intensive educational curriculum involving a pre-med undergraduate degree, a four year professional program, and an internship and residency emphasizing foot surgery, biomechanics, and sports medicine.

D.P.M.'s must pass state and national licensing exams which are monitored by the American Academy of Podiatric Sports Medicine (AAPSM). The academy also is active in promoting and presenting research on podiatric sports medicine.

To learn more about the field and attain a copy of the professional magazine the academy publishes, contact:

American Academy of Podiatric Sports Medicine
1729 Glastonberry Road
Potomac, MD 20854

(301) 424-7440

Presently, there are no colleges per se for the education of sports podiatry. However, a list of the colleges of podiatric medicine is as follows:

California College of Podiatric Medicine
Box 7855
San Francisco, CA 94120

College of Podiatric Medicine & Surgery
University of Osteopathic Medicine
3200 Grand Avenue
Des Moines, IA 50312

College of Podiatric Medicine
1001 N. Dearborn Avenue
Chicago, IL 60610

Pennsylvania College of Podiatric Medicine
Eighth and Race Streets
Philadelphia, PA 19107

The future of podiatry will continue to be bright as earnings for D.P.M.'s should range from $40,000 to $80,000 annually depending on the size and location of the practice or clinic.

*The NATA also publishes the fine NATA JOURNAL, *Athletic Training.* This publication provides excellent information on athletic training and sports medicine advancements.

Other Sports Related Careers

There are numerous sports opportunities in fields which assist sports medicine practitioners but are not able to sustain a full-time business with sports clients. Technicians in sports prosthetics and orthotics are frequently being called upon to develop and design knee and elbow braces, foot supports, body jackets, and on occasion custom tailor protective equipment during injury rehabilitation.

These "design experts" work closely with sports medicine personnel for the purpose of providing injury prevention mechanisms that will not alter performance. Few technicians will exclusively work with athletics, but for those wishing to learn more of the rewarding and at times financially successful career, contact your local sports medicine clinic or write:

The American Orthotic & Prosthetic Association
717 Pendleton Street
Alexandria, VA 22314

Other professionals whose specialized services are sought by athletes include dentists and the eye care experts, optometrists and ophthalmologists.

The input of dentists into the design of mouthpieces and faceguards has seen a reduction in the number of injuries to the mouth area by nearly 60%.

Sports vision consultants on the other hand believe that the vision system directs the muscular system, thus allowing the successful athlete to have a greater reaction system. It is this innate reaction system that some feel determines an athlete's ability.

In either case, both fields are vital to the physical care and performance levels of competitors. If you would like to learn more about these educationally demanding yet interesting professions, write:

American Dental Association
211 East Chicago Avenue
Chicago, IL 60611

American Optometric Association
243 North Lindburg Boulevard
St. Louis, MO 63141

Sports Medicine Paraprofessionals

For each professional practitioner there is at least one support staff member that will assist in a variety of capacities. These paraprofessionals are trained health aids who are permitted to perform numerous functions once previously undertaken by the doctor, or physical therapist.

A career as an assistant will usually involve a short yet intense formal training program in the related sports medicine field. All of the preceding sports medicine professionals mentioned thus far utilize paraprofessionals in their practices. Many of these paraprofessionals will later choose to further themselves as professional practitioners.

Entrance into any one of the sports medicine paraprofessional fields is not difficult and the education involved can last as short as 6 months to 2 years. Hourly wages paid to assistants will range with an income in the neighborhood of $12,000-$16,000 per year.

The job outlook for paraprofessionals remains good as it should experience a steady increase in the numbers needed in the years ahead.

Sports Massage

The newest and fastest developing concept seen in the sports medicine field is the art of massage. Body massage treatments are considered to be therapeutic and have been clinically proven to be successful in relieving mental & physical strain, in assisting as a complementary procedure during injury rehabilitation, and in preventing possible injury through its stretching and flexibility principles. Sports masseurs and masseuses have been extensively called upon by both individual athletes and race organizers to perform their services at triathalons, marathons, and track events.

Athletes are not the only ones who have experienced the benefits of body massage as mental health centers and hospital clinics are increasingly adding these specialists to their therapy staffs. However the majority of massage artists are in private practice with their own exclusive clientele. Once a reputation has been established, a good masseur or masseuse can earn anywhere from $20.00 to $45.00 per hourly session.

The practice of massage is strictly a therapeutic process and should not be viewed as a recreational service. Though certification is not required as of yet, the formal training involved is quite extensive. As far as the future for employment is concerned, the market is wide open for men and women practitioners.

Two institutions of noted notoriety for their specialized training are as follows:

The Sports Massage Training Institute

The nation's most comprehensive training program in the rapidly expanding field of Sports Massage.

The SMTI program includes pre, post and preventive massage, injury care, trigger point, P.N.F. stretches, clinical internship . . . and more.

SMTI publishes the Sports Massage Journal and is recognized world wide as a leader of sports massage training. Call or write for a free brochure:

The Sports Massage Training Institute of Encinitas
121 West "E" Street
Encinitas, CA 92024
(619) 942-6128

Minneapolis School of Massage

The philosophy of the sports massage program is that the human body needs to be in balance to prevent injury and optimize performance. A student who wishes to be certified in the 12 week sports massage work must first complete training in the basic 2 week massage course. A unique concept of this program is that students may proceed at their own pace of study before completing an internship with the local Division I college athletic training department. For more information, contact:

Jim Traver
Minneapolis School of Massage, 23 SE 4th St.
Minneapolis, MN 55414
(612) 623-7616

CHAPTER 9

COMMUNICATIONS & MASS MEDIA

Without communications, sports undoubtedly would have never achieved the status it enjoys today. Take away the print and electronic media, which have provided the public with information and publicity on athletic events, and possibly all who would be interested in sports would be just the participants themselves. Also, if it weren't for the financial sponsorships provided by network broadcasting, many of today's sports franchises would be unable to stay in existence much less show a profit. The athletes themselves have the mass media to thank for indirectly allowing them to receive salaries that at one time would be nothing more than a far fetched fantasy.

An excellent example of the benefits television revenue produces can be illustrated by examining a professional hockey team. Due to a lack of media sponsorship, many NHL clubs must charge in excess of $20.00 per ticket for their 41 home contests only to discover that they still may not be able to break even financially. In contrast, an NFL franchise may not need to depend on ticket sales for revenue since each organization is awarded $16 million for broadcasting rights before the season even begins. Imagine where professional soccer could be if they were to receive such a lucrative television pact!

An indepth look at the historical evolution and movement of sport clearly gives rise to the impact the mass media has played in popularizing sport. In the early 1900s college football was strictly a regional sport played predominantly in the east while it also wasn't until as late as the 1950s that major league baseball news extended west of the Mississippi River. Advancements in communications have changed both scenarios as football interest has reached epidemic proportions nationwide and baseball has become America's #1 pastime.

The influx of expanded wire services, an increase in the usage of radio broadcasting, and the onset of television programming have made sports more visible in the eyes and ears of the general public. The interest in sports generated by the media ultimately led to a demand for the development of new leagues and franchises.

However, sports coverage in the 80s has blossomed to the point where many marketing experts believe that a certain degree of overexposure exists within particular sports. An oversaturated product can lead to eventual disinterest if not kept in perspective.

No one knows better of such ramifications to overexposure than the producers of NFL Monday Night Football and the organizers of the now defunct USFL. It was the belief that the football fan could never see enough coverage on television, as the former expanded television coverage to additional evenings and the latter employed a spring schedule. Obviously, both failed in this rationale as seen with poor viewer ratings resulting in a subsequent loss of broadcasting dollars, and for the USL, the lack of any television contracts led to the league's demise.

In any event, sports media personnel have become as familiar as the athletes themselves and for many, they enjoy a much more lasting career than the sports performers. No longer is the reporter a "behind the scenes" person as each journalist has developed a personal sphere of attention. It isn't uncommon for a sports enthusiast to watch a particular telecast, tune in a particular radio station or read a selected column just to be entertained or amused by the coverage of the event from a favorite reporter or telecaster.

As glamorous as this life may seem, so are the demands and frustrations in this fast paced line of work. The competition to be a part of this scene is fierce, but for the fan that will succeed to the top, the satisfaction and benefits can be quite rewarding.

Newspapers

Sportswriting represents the oldest and still the most basic component of athletic journalism. No matter what member of the sports media you may talk to, in all likelihood that person had a start by writing in one form or another. There is no substitute for sound writing skills, the ability to ferret out facts and separate them from fiction, the dedication and enthusiasm towards attaining perfection, and, of course, a sense of humor. Without these attributes, it is doubtful that the aspiring reporter has much of a chance to make it to the "big time."

There are several schools of thought in which route to pursue in becoming a newspaper sportswriter. The advantage of a small newspaper provides the opportunity to be involved in every facet of the busines — writing, reporting, editing, laying out, and even photography. In a sense, learning the "nuts and bolts" from the basic levels can be sort of a proving grounds to see if this is what you truly desire as a career endeavor.

Still there are others who believe that once a position can be attained in a major metropolitan newspaper, the possibility for advancement will greatly increase. It should be pointed out that a majority of all applicants will take this approach. The main advantage here is that newspapers in metropolitan areas will provide the opportunity to cover highly visible events in addition to being able to create a media identity through the vast numbers that read the sports section.

In any case, try to acquire as much experience as possible, even if it is for gratis. Remember what was stated earlier in this publication, "If you are good enough, someone will discover you."

In the career development chapter, it was pointed out how lifestyle should be considered when contemplating a lifelong career. Sportswriting careers are no exception in this evaluation. Being a tireless worker in this field does not mean just the length in hours, but also should be equated with working long hours during weekends, nights, and even holidays. If you are assigned to cover a baseball or hockey team, a considerable amount of your time will be spent on the road, sometimes not in the most desirable climates or populated locations.

Training

Athletes are told that if they are to be proficient performers, they must talk, eat, and sleep every aspect of their chosen sport. The same holds true for sportswriters as they need to be a sports historian of sorts constantly reading publications and talking the language of sport. Specialized courses such as the geography of sport help prepare the "trivia expert" to understand the concept of sport more fully. So many of today's sports enthusiasts don't seem to understand that the history of sport did not begin with Peter Rose or Wayne Gretzky, but began in Greece and somewhere along the way came the Cy Younjgs and the Red Granges.

The point to be made here is that a writer needs to put an event or individual feat into perspective within the total picture of the sport. How often do we hear sports media people proclaim a team, a game, or an accomplishment as being of an ''all-time'' magnitude when in actuality if the competition, the conditions, or the technological advancements were taken into account, the feat may have not been so remarkable. Who knows, maybe if there was as much media exposure then as there is now, we would be better equipped to make such comparisons.

In addition to acquiring ''street knowledge'' of sports, without the proper formal education there can possibly be no future in any segment of communications. An undergraduate degree in journalism is highly recommended, but majors in English, literature, or sports sciences with a writing minor could suffice. It can be said that you cannot really learn to write — only to write better.

Experience

Don't think for a minute that all a sportswriter does is watch a game and report on it. That's the easy part and the least time consuming. Developing a style, transposing events into words, and making an article entertaining is the real ''art'' of writing. There's only one way to fine tune those already-existing skills which cannot be taught, and that's by constantly refining them through experience.

Working for a high school or college daily paper, a local neighborhood publication, or even freelancing can provide the necessary opportunities to develop your talents. After all, even by serving in the capacity as a non-compensated staff member, you possibly may be given a press pass to cover major events which could lead to contacts and other future assignments.

Wire Services

The other area of opportunity a sports journalist may choose to pursue is that of a wire service reporter. In actuality, this route serves as the best possible training ground for becoming a newspaper sportswriter since it will require the journalist to perform under tremendous pressure to be efficient and accurate. Additionally, wire service reporters must also have a sound knowledge of all sports considering that the essence of time restraints will not allow them to be able to pick the story of their choice.

Working under the many pressured deadlines will at times necessitate reporters to dictate their stories forcing them to rely on keen thinking and instinctual fact finding. The only drawback here is that the story may appear to lack literary style causing one to believe that the report is not of a professional nature. Unfortunately, though not ture, this is one of the the raps many wire service writers must learn to cope with.

As opposed to the staff writer, who may only write one story of a given day, a wire service reporter could be assigned to work on an advance story on an upcoming contest, cover the game itself, return to the office to report on the event, and possibly be assigned to complete another advance story all in the same day! Needless to say, the workloads between the two journalism positions have quite a variance, but the process of accomplishing the tasks of a wire service reporter will prove to be invaluable in the long run.

No matter what route you may choose, the typical day in each will present new challenges to a reporter that will not allow him/her to live on past accomplishments. The advantage to this work style is that despite what may happen, positive or negative, there will always be a tomorrow to prove yourself.

Writers will not always come across to the public as heroes and by maintaining a strong sense of objectivity, they possibly could become very unpopular figures. On occasion reporters may

80

have no choice but to ask questions or report on incidents that the public may not want to know. You must always keep in mind that journalists are employed by the newspaper or wire service, not by a school, coach, or organization.

At the same time you cannot let personal biases cloud your work as a professional. In other words, there is no room to be a fan much less have personal favorites. And as one last precaution, don't break the cardinal rule of taking bribes or providing preferential coverage. There will be too many other hungry writers willing to step in and report the facts "as is," and once you have an established reputation, it will stick with you wherever you go.

The future for print journalists remains good but due to the competitiveness of the field, many jobs will offer minimal pay scales. The writer's guild, to which a reporter is a member, will dictate the salary structure that will be administered. For the most part, earnings will be in the $13,000 to $35,000 range depending on the size of the publication, experience, and the writer's guild. Freelancing for publications and magazines can prove to be very profitable, but the financial rewards will not be attainable until you have established your own writing style and reputation.

Organizations that may provide additional insight into this career field are as follows:

American Council on Education for Journalism
563 Essex Court
Deerfield, IL 60015
(312) 948-5840

Associated Press Sports Editors Association
St. Petersburg Times
St. Petersburg, FL 33731
(813) 893-8111

National Federation of Press Women
1006 Main Street
P.O. Box 99
Blue Springs, MO 64015
(816) 229-1666

Television

Without a doubt, television represents the pinnacle of success in the sports mass media. Not only are the many media related positions seen as prestigious and glamorous, but the salaries in this segment of communications can reach the heights of highly paid athletes.

Even though the on-the-air personalities are the most recognizable members of any sports telecast, there are numerous "behind the scenes" personnel functions ranging from directors, producers, and cameramen, to stage managers, artists, and technicians, that make a sports broadcast possible.

Since the majority of aspiring journalists target television as their career endeavor, the competition to enter the market will be extremely fierce with only a select few ever realizing their dreams. A misconception many students of sports have is that the only sure fire way of attaining a broadcasting position is to be an ex-athlete. Though this is true in as far as getting a foot in the door, but how many ex-"jocks" do you ever see having their network contracts renewed or ever succeed beyond the role as a color commentator? The point to be made is that a name cannot carry the audience's attention, but the dynamics of the presentation will.

If there is such a thing as a sportscaster type per se, this person would undoubtedly be attractive, wellspoken, and would be able to convey an upbeat, energetic personality. Even though there is a definite need to amuse and stimulate the viewing public, sportscasters must understand that they are to be journalists first and entertainers second.

Besides projecting a positive image, sportscasters must know how to utilize the English language almost artlike in making concise yet flowing statements. Becoming a trivia expert is not important since sports information or public relations departments can provide any necessary statistics. The farm more important task is to be able to translate what is seen and present the happenings in an understandable and interesting format. The sportscaster then should be looked upon by the viewing audience as the action's interpreter.

Due to the instinctive nature a play-by-play sportscaster must possess during a telecast, countless hours of preparation must take place days before the event. This may include studying team profiles, interviewing players, or even memorizing numbers. A sportscaster becomes an instantaneous reporter without the luxury of editing words and sentences in order for them to flow cohesively. This is the major difference between a play-by-play sportscaster and a color commentator who will have the opportunity to rehearse a statement or summary momentarily before making an analysis. This is why so many sportscasters begin as "color man" since it won't require to be as reactive initially.

Getting Started

Without a doubt there is an element of luck in landing *any* broadcasting position. There are several schools of thought in how to prepare oneself and establish a successful track record, but no one strategy should be considered more noteworthy than the other.

As has been previously mentioned, a strong background in journalism and communications represents the foundation of any aspiring sportscaster. There are universities that offer specialized training in the television arts while some may even have their own television stations allowing for the additional opportunity of "hands on" experience.

Some of today's most heralded media figures have begun their careers in a similar fashion. Brent Musburger of CBS is a graduate of Northwestern University. After majoring in journalism, he worked as a sportswriter before shortly turning to television. Vin Scully, who is especially known for his work as a football and baseball broadcaster, was one of Fordham University's first graduates in its communication arts program. He was hired as the voice of the Brooklyn Dodgers right off the college campus some 30 years ago. There are many other major network sportscasters who had their roots in an educational setting who were fortunate enough to be given internships or temporary positions on account of their formal training.

Some of the universities that have established advanced curriculums in the television arts include Illinois, UCLA, Syracuse, and Missouri. For those wishing to attend a more specialized and accelerated training program, there do exist broadcasting schools for students with such targeted goals.

The most widely acclaimed institute that has an established reputation in mass communications is as follows:

Brown Institute
The Brown Institute, which is one of the most well-known radio-television broadcasting schools, is located in Minneapolis, Minnesota. Brown was founded in 1946 and currently has graduates employed in radio and television from coast to coast.

Entrance requirements include a special voice and reading analysis with new classes beginning quarterly. Flexible schedules allow students to attend evening sessions while many graduates complete their classes in as little time as 36 weeks.

Brown has recently initiated an 18 month associate degree program which is geared towards individuals without a college background. The associate degree program includes college level general education courses in economics, sociology, and psychology, in addition to advanced broadcasting courses.

The average Brown Institute graduate steps up regularly in salary and often moves to larger stations and more responsible positions. The school's placement service assists graduates nationwide with many securing positions with the leading radio, television, and cable networks. Many graduates who prefer administrative work now own their own broadcasting stations.

Radio-television broadcasting students who have completed at least eight weeks may take the Sports Course at the same time. Play-by-play experience involves one or two major sports located in the Twin Cities area depending on the time of year the student wishes to attend.

For more information on this exciting field, contact:

Mike Mullen
Chairman - National Education of Broadcasting
Brown Institute Campus
3123 East Lake Street
Minneapolis, Minnesota 55406

(612) 721-2481

Upon completion of a formal education program, there are two basic directions to pursue in the sportscasting profession: as a play-by-play announcer or as a sportscaster on a television station news show. There are those sportscasters who have duo roles whereby they perform both at the station and have contracts enabling them to also work games at the college or professional level. But for the most part, the ideal situation would be to broadcast in only one aspect of the profession.

Despite the various paths and strategies that have proven to be successful by many of today's leading broadcasters, it should be assumed that a vast majority of the inexperienced media professionals will start their careers in a smaller market or outlying area and eventually apsire to secure a position with a larger city or station. Though this approach may appear to be somewhat unpromising and vague, it cannot be over emphasized that the competition to be a part of this field, especially in the larger markets, has left little in alternatives but to go somewhere else no matter how desolate the location in order to create an identity. Some impatient and ambitious enterpreneurs have taken matters into their own hands by starting or buying their own broadcasting stations thus guaranteeing the opportunity tobe on the air. Though costly, this route does provide a considerable amount of room to be creative.

In any advent, the outlook for sports broadcasting remains fair at most. Salaries for top network play-by-play sports people can exceed $500,000 or more while "color" commentators can receive anywhere from $25,000 per telecast. As far as studio sports directors go, a major metropolitan station may compensate their sportscaster to the tune of $100,000. But here again, the size of the market will have the greatest bearing on the salary structure. No better is this illustrated than with independent stations where it is not uncommon for telecasters to be renumerated for as little as $100.00 for a college basketball game.

Organizations that may provide additional information include the following:

National Association of Broadcasters
1771 North Street N.W.
Washington, D.C. 20036

(202) 293-3500

National Sportscasters and Sportswriters Association
P.O. Drawer 559
Salisburg, NC 28144

(704) 633-4275

Television Support Personnel

To this point only the sportscasters have been outlined in the varied career opportunities that exist in television broadcasting. But as has been already mentioned at the onset of this section, on-the-air people comprise only a small fraction of the total staff necessary to telecast a sporting event.

What few sports minded individuals realize is that there are positions available in television that will incorporate aspects of nearly every career interest or personality type. From the blue collar worker who possesses electronic skills to the white collar individual who has creative abilities, there will always be a demand for "people oriented" producers and sophisticated technical personnel at both the local and network levels.

Producers & Directors

As the overseers to any televised sporting event, producers will coordinate the coverage of a contest which will also include preparation of the announcers, production crew, and technical staff on the mechanics of how and what must take place.

Even though the producer may have a set game plan going into any production, the "crew" may experience a degree of frustration or uneasiness during the telecast since they will ultimately be unable to control the happenings during the game. No matter how much preparation goes into an event, there are many unpredictable variables such as weather, overtimes, injuries, etc. will have a hand in the coverage strategy.

The major difference between a producer and a director is whereas a producer pulls the total production together, the director will execute the finer elements of the telecast. What this translates into is that a director will call all the shots as to what pictures and replays will appear on the screen and if necessary troubleshoot situations (i.e. mistakes made by the announcers or time lags that may affect the quality of the show).

There are many skills that are necessary to perform either of these roles proficiently. Not only must one possess developed organizational and administrative abilities, but even more importantly, this person must understand the necessity of attention to details. Putting together a sports program will involve right to the second accurateness. Considering that Super Bowl advertisements can run as high as $500,000 for each minute of air time, the slightest miscalculation can result in foregone coverage of the game or even worse; litigation by one of the sponsors for not meeting contractual time lengths.

Having and extensive sports background along with a sound sense of what is transpiring on the playing field are intangibles that cannot be substituted with any other form of experience. It is almost as if the "crew" must be thinking in the same terms as the coach or manager in order to anticipate plays or strategy. By using such objectiveness and instantaneous judgment, the network could be spared of any embarrassment resulting from one of those unexpected occurrences in which the technicians were left flat footed.

A first step in preparing oneself for a career in television production would be to acquire a thorough knowledge of communications and the mass media. It is never too early to gain exposure to all kinds of sporting contests and develop people handling skills. This can be attained while even attending school or like most major network producers, by becoming involved with a local television station. If possible, it may be even more beneficial to be associated with a cable station or independent network that specializes in local sports coverage since all of your time then will be strictly related to athletics.

Television producers are handsomely compensated and it is not uncommon for a network producer to earn in upwards of $275,000 annually. It has also been the case where production staff members can equal the earnings of those "on-the-air" specialists.

Cameramen

On-site cameramen are known as the "men in the trenches" in the television industry. No matter what the conditions, heat, cold, or snow, they are required to perform at the same level of competence as if they were in the studio.

Like the producer, the camera technician must be able to have a feel for the sport being telecasted as well as being able to anticipate and often stay ahead of the commands from the control booth. Even with preplanned camera coverage, situations will arise in which only the alert technician will be able to provide indepth coverage to the viewing audience. It is in these instances that award winning film clips and videos are made or become trademarks of the industry.

The training for such a line of work is usually available at area technical schools and usually can be completed in a relative short period of time. Some programs even offer intern programs in which students can be hired upon completion of their education.

But for the most part, cameramen will begin their careers at a local station or cable company before being sought by a major sports market.

Salaries will vary depending upon past assignments and the size of the employing television station. A first-time cameraman can expect a salary figure in the upper teens while a seasoned technician can usually demand a figure in the neighborhood of $25,000 per year.

Radio

Without a doubt, radio broadcasting presents the best overall opportunities in the sports mass media market in as far as a quick entry with rapid advancement are concerned. In fact those sportscasters who have become successful in the television sector nearly all had their beginnings with radio. Since radio is primarily a local medium, and taking into account the countless number of stations that exist even in the most desolate of areas, the possibilities for employment are endless.

Radio can also be utilized as a training period before moving into a larger market or television for that matter. This is not to say that the competition is any less, only that the initial upward movements are much more readily attainable in radio as compared to television sportscasting.

As any other communications position, a fine command of the English language is vital and possibly even more so here since radio reports do not have the luxury of a television picture to describe the action. It will take patience, experience, and nurturing to be able to allow the listener to actually visualize and be a part of the scene by your description.

A shortcoming many young radio reporters possess is an inability to listen especially to details given by the athlete when being interviewed. Listening attentively is an art and by not doing so effectively, pertinent newsworthy information or the establishment of rapport with a player could be lost as a result.

As far as training is concerned, many schools and vocational institutes offer what usually are short-termed curriculums. The Brown Institute described earlier has developed one of the finest reputations in the country for this field.

Radio broadcasting does not provide as lucrative of a compensation structure as its television counterpart, but does however offer a wider range of job availability.

When securing a position, there are some professional franchises and collegiate teams that do hire their own "voice" to do their telecasts, but the more customary route is to secure employment at a local sports station. There is one added tradeoff for radio in that the radio voice for a team is many times more popular and often heard than the sportscaster who is involved with the play-by-play on television.

The earnings for a radio sportscaster can vary immensely depending on the size of the station and the duties involved. Some reporters have their own shows as well as announce daily updates while others only broadcast a specific sport and may freelance at other assignments. In any case, radio reports can expect to receive as low as $10,000 to as high as $100,000 annually.

Sports Photography

Even in sports there is an appreciation for an artist, especially the photographer who can capture a single action of an athlete or play and raise it to dramatic proportions. Whether it be the intensity on the face of a tennis server or the exasperation expressed after a missed opportunity, how true it is that a single picture can speak 1,000 words.

While the reporter may labor over phrases and words to describe a feeling or expression, the photographer can put the whole story into perspective with just one click of the shutter.

Most sports photographers can have their beginnings traced back to their high school yearbook days or college newspaper experiences. It's never too early to start much less provide or even sell select action shots to local neighborhood newspapers or publications.

Like so many other artful professions, there is little informal photography training, just fine tuning clinics and seminars. However it will be necessary to put together a portfolio of your work to demonstrate your abilities. Like the television technician, there will be no substitute for experience or knowledge of the sport you are covering. Many of the premier sports photographers have found it valuable to know the personalities and the action setters of each sport. Being at the right place at the right time can be all you will ever need. A fine example of this is the famed Dwight Clark catch inthe endzone of the 1982 NFL playoffs to allow the San Francisco 49ers to beat the Dallas Cowboys in the waning moments. How often do we see that one shot duplicated time and time again?

Being in photography is much like public relations and marketing. Getting your work to be bought and published will require a certain element of "hustling." By developing your own prints, you will be much better adept at putting together contact sheets not to mention having a more cost effective business.

The outlook for sports photographers remains good as the more popular choice of freelancing can be much more profitable once you have learned the tricks of the trade by serving on a newspaper or school staff. Don't specialize in only one sport; in fact, it may be even more advantageous to cover the many so-called "minor sports." Since few photographers have prints of these sports, when the need does arise to do a feature, you will be able to provide the necessary photos and possibly get a foot in the door.

Many choose sports photography as an avocation but for those who do pursue this interest on a full-time basis, earnings can vary from $10,000 to $35,000 a year. This career can also provide an excellent side income for those photographers who have their own businesses (i.e. weddings and portraits) and contract their services to local high schools, colleges, and professional teams.

To learn more about this field or photography in general, contact:

Photographic Society of America
P.O. Box 1266
Reseda, CA 91335

CHAPTER 10

SPORTS CAREERS AND POSITIONS

The business of sport is simply another form of the entertainment industry which revolves around a uniquely talented group of people - athletes.

People who involve themselves in the highly visible environment of sports as a life's occupation should also learn to accept their chosen game's peculiar nuances, the structure of its rules, and its sometimes overly egotistical and demanding performing entertainers. Even more important, individuals entering athletic related fields should be prepared to work for more than just monetary compensation. Sports practitioners should be willing to put something more of themselves into their chosen endeavor not only for their own good or the good of the perspective oranization, but also for the preservation and enhancement of sport itself.

The upcoming listings of sports careers are a far cry fom the 9 to 5 existence found in many other non-athletic settings. What will be encountered are long nights, weekends, holidays, and often endless hours which go unnoticed by the public whose only interest is in winners or losers. It is the hope of this author that readers share a common desire to be in the spirit of their team or organization and work devotedly towards establishing ethical standards and creating a sense of loyalty and commitment to a cause.

Since it may be assumed that success is directly proportionate to the amount of time that is put forth into a chosen field, then a successful career in sports is formulated no differently than any non-sports career. The difference in which an individual may pursue a sports career more tanaciously may be attributed to the flare and excitement that can't be rewarded or experienced as in the sports arena compared to other walks of life. As long as there is a ball to be thrown or kicked, a rink or gridiron to be practiced on, and considering the premium American society places on competition and physical prowess, there always will be new and developing opportunities in sports and athletics.

Professional Athletes

Phil Niekro Sr., the ageless pitcher for the New York Yankees, commented on his sons - Phil Jr. and Joe, both professional baseball players, "I'm proud of them and happy that they don't have to work for a living."

The foremost category of sport careers is that of the professional athlete. Take away the athletes and there are no more sports much less any of the various occupations that involve sport personnel. Never has there been a society where athletes possess the notoriety and acquire the prosperity as there now exists in the United States. This fast becomes even more obvious with the growing numbers of European and even Soviet bloc athletes that continue to seek professional contracts in soccer, hockey, and tennis. What other country can offer its athletically gifted people the opportunity to obtain a college education which may lead to millionaire status at a tender young age, not to mention the many business propositions that may evolve from playing professionally?

Since the professional athlete has become the number one American hero adored by young and old alike, it is no wonder that youngsters emulate the every move of the athlete they see on television and in person. Disadvantaged youths view professional sports as a quick route to "easy street" mistaking the wealth and fame of a select few athletes as a representation of the norm for all professional athletes. This unsatiable quest to become a professional performer is usually pursued at the expense of formal education and normal career development which if put into perspective, it is the educational process that provides the only real hope for any lasting, successful future. Dr. Harry Edwards, a California sports sociologist, believes the disadvantaged and black youths would benefit more by emulating and following the career paths of black doctors and lawyers. His belief is based on the premise that these fields are readily more atttainable for minorities considering that the odds in numbers alone of being successful favor these professionals as opposed to athletics and that scholarships and grants are also more available in these areas, since there is a shortage of black practitioners and students.

Arthur Ashe wrote this provocative statement to black parents:

> There must be some way to assure that the 999 who try but don't make it to pro sports don't wind up on the street corners or in the unemployment lines. Unfortunately, our most widely recognized role models are athletes and entertainers — "runnin" and "jumpin" and "singin" and "dancin." While we are 60 percent of the National Basketball Association, we are less than 4 percent of the doctors and lawyers. While we are about 35 percent of major league baseball, we are less than 2 percent of the engineers. While we are about 40 percent of the National Football League, we are less than 11 percent of construction workers such as carpenters and bricklayers.
>
> Our greatest heroes of the century have been athletes — Jack Johnson, Joe Lewis, and Muhammad Ali. Racial and economic discrimination forced us to channel our energies into athletics and entertainment. These are the ways out of the ghetto, the ways to get the Cadillac, those alligator shoes, the cashmere sport coat.
>
> Somehow, parents must instill a desire for learning alongside the desire to be Walt Frazier. Why not start by sending black professional athletes into high schools to explain the facts of life. I have often addressed high school audiences and my message is always the same. For every hour you spend on the athletic field spend two in the library. Even if you make it as a pro athlete, your career will be over by the time you are tirty-five. So you will need this diploma.

To further delude the picture of professional playing careers, that with a stroke of a pen, an unproven, 22-year old without a college degree, has the possibility of becoming an instant millionaire with fringe benefits comparable to any tenured corporate executive!

But can professional athletics actually be considered a viable career when considering that the average longevity of a professional sports figure is only 4½ years? Put into simpler terms, that by the time a young person has reached his 27th birthday, his professional playing days have come to a halt, many times without a legitimate career alternative to fall back on to create a new identity.

Where once pro sports were looked upon as an opportunity to continue competition and establish a financial base before entering a permanent occupation, now competition has given head way to the importance of extravagant wealth and high living. Unfortunately, financial security, with the ability to retire early, can rarely be accomplished in most pro careers.

Athletes aspiring a pro status should keep "playing" goals in perspective and remain realistic about their individual talents. In football and basketball, drafted college players must usually "make it" during their first season or forget about any future considerations. Comparing the professional systems utilized in baseball and hockey, young enthusiasts must be prepared to spend developmental time in the minor leagues on the average of 5 years. The longer the time spent in the junior circuits, the more reduced the chances become of reaching the major leagues or parent franchises. In other sports such as golf, tennis, or bowling, the road to success isn't as well defined. These sports implicate processes that involve either apprenticeship programs to develop professionals, attendance at schools offering specialized training for those wishing to qualify for the professional tours, or sponsorships that provide financial stability for unranked or non-prize winning competitors.

Whichever route is chosen for the appropriate sport, the odds are against you — probably 140,000 to 1 when comparing the average yearly number of active youth participants to the actual total of athletes performing at the professional level. Granted, the odds will vary immensely from sports of national popularity such as baseball to activities of relative minority interest like figure skating, but the fact still remains that during a normal season, only 1200 players are rostered in the NFL, 400 in the NHL, and at the most, 100 boxers compete professionally.

What It Takes To Be A Pro

Without a doubt, the major prerequisite to attaining professional playing status is physical ability. If a person has the tools for a specific sport, then he/she, if they so desire, will play somewhere — period. How often is it seen where an athlete may have trained and played at a particular position during their scholastic career only to be moved to a new skill position upon being drafted professionally. If the natural skills are present, athletes may even be chosen by a sport that they either have had little playing experience in or have no longer been a participant. Dave Winfield, outfielder for the New York Yankees, was selected during both baseball's and basketball's professional draft due to his illustrious collegiate career in both sports at the University of Minnesota. What has rarely been publicized is the fact that he was also chosen on the 17th round in the NFL's selection process despite never playing football in college.

An NFL personnel director sums it up best by stating, "You can accomplish a great deal with a burning desire to play and by becoming an overachiever, but the first step to success is inevitably possessing the ability to compete proficiently at the professional level."

Another key element sought by team scouts in potential pros is instinct, better known as "street sense." An athlete that exhibits this trait has the "feel" for a given performance situation in which he/she can recognize and act accordingly without the need to be overly analytical. Many times this reaction is a reflex with the physical skills responding to a mental trigger. Athletes possessing this talent are the "big play" people who seem to have the uncanny knack to turn a game around with their individual skills. Some of the greatest clutch players of all time really didn't possess on paper the statistics representative of an overachiever. Brooks Robinson, former 3rd baseman for the Baltimore Orioles, never had an extraordinary high lifetime batting average or fielding percentage. But with runners in scoring position when his team was behind or if the situation called for a double play to be turned to squelch a rally, the man you wanted to be at bat or have the ball hit to was Brooks. His "give me the ball" attitude will long be remembered as his trademark, not his overall batting average. The instinctive intelligence that has been exemplified to this point cannot be learned in a book or even coached. If this natural gift is not existent in a performer, then it will need to be overcompensated for with a higher development of the individual's physical and mental talents.

Intelligence may also be viewed as the knowledge and understanding of what it takes to be a winner; accepting roles that may be for the good of the team rather than the self; the importance of "respecting" one's own body through proper conditioning and nutrition; and "giving it all" each time the clock starts or the umpire calls "play ball." This notion of intelligence has provided the foundation for a minority of veterans who in their 40's still continue to perform flawlessly while others have fallen victim to the statistic of a 4½ year playing career. Pete Rose, now coach for the Cincinnati Reds, epitomizes the spirit of the game with his remarkable, yet never ending resilience. Rose believes there are two necessary ingredients for continued success through the course of a season — enthusiasm and aggressiveness. Given these characteristics along with the ability to play major league calibre ball, there is no limit to what may be accomplished in the eyes of a coach such as Pete Rose.

It is important, too, to realize at a young age what sport best fits your personality, style and physical capacities. Many athletes find themselves excelling at one sport and at times floundering or continually being frustrated in another. This is why the emergence of sports psychologists and biomechanists has become so valuable. Technicians in these fields can discover which athletic events are best suited for each individual to attain maximal performance. Whether you are more inclined to compete individually or cooperate in a team setting, or your body performs more efficiently in endurance events as opposed to short spurt activities, finding your natural tendencies may enable you to choose a sport that is both more satisfying and productive.

Even if you have already spent years of endless training in a particular sport and now find it wasn't meant to be your niche in life, counseling and testing by professionals may provide more effective training guidelines in addition to possibly redirecting deficient mental facilities to enhance overall performance.

Professional athletes who compete only for the financial rewards will rarely be consistent winners in the long run. Players must incorporate a sense of team and individual pride along with exhibiting unselfish sacrifices to be successful in a team event. For those athletes who view professional sports as a means to financial security, there later may exist a feeling of inner frustration that they were never truly fulfilled as the competitor. Being called a "professional" athlete involves a responsibility of being just what the word implicates — being professional. In the eyes of the sports fan, the most admired professional athletes as those who are not only skilled, but are equally able to utilize very ounce of ability in making themselves better. To begin in the right direction, aspiring pros should examine the lifestyles of athletes who exhibit a love for their team and the game while consistently maintaining a touch of class. Observe what has made successful athletes successful and institute these traits as role models in your own professional pursuit.

One of the major transitions encountered by most young athletes is that of adjusting from amateur to professional status. No longer will athletes be given preferential treatment over others like so many once were accustomed to in high school and college. The professional team or organization, unlike many university programs, does not need to concern itself with keeping people eligible academically much less provide financial favors in order for athletes to choose their team over another. Since the bottom line now is to win at all costs, student rights are replaced with a contract that mandates performing despite the physical, social or emotional state present at game time. A former pro-athlete puts pro sports into perspective by comparing the one major factor that isn't present in amateur or collegiate sports. Simply stated, "one must learn to accept and play with pain and adversity on a daily basis."

Comparably speaking, the seasons are longer, the stakes become higher, and the travel is more extensive no matter which sport is chosen. Performing a skill to perfection is not the standard to gauge excellence, but executing successfully day-in and day-out will eventually separate the haves from the have nots. The emotional and mental burn-out so commonly seen today has been the antagonist in the termination of many otherwise potentially prosperous careers. Remember too, it is not whether or not an athlete can kick a 63-yard field goal in practice or land a triple jump during a figure skating routine, but can the same feat be duplicated time and time again under the most highly pressured situations?

One national sports magazine considered this following statement by Olympic medalist Mary Lou Retten to be the "Best Sports Quote of 1984." Mary Lou remarks, "Here's what it takes to be a complete gymnast. Someone should be able to sneak up and drag you out at midnight, push you out on some strange floor — and you should be able to do your entire routine sound asleep in your pajamas. *Without one mistake.* That's the secret. It's got to be a natural reaction."

While it may appear premature to discuss life after sports when a playing career has yet to materialize, it is equally important to prepare oneself for the probable let down as well as discovering what it takes to go on to a more complete and fulfilling existence. So often the sports pages will report how ex-jocks are unable to rejoin the "real world" after retirement and are experiencing maladjustments with their personal lives. In retrospect, this behavior is to be somewhat expected since the better part of an athlete's life has been spent being foundled by a public which has a thirst to worship heros and be near celebrities. This lack of a normal existence is compounded by an almost cult-like relationship developed with fellow teammates who together have survived unique stress situations rarely experienced in other walks of life. Letting go of this form of shared comradery is a difficult adjustment especially when considering it has represented the one support group that proved to be so vital when things went wrong and others could not understand.

Even though it is not easy to match an experience such as playing in front of a national audience in quest of a world championship, there is more to a person than playing sports for a few years. Those who are unable to grasp the concept are only shortchanging themselves of totally fulfilling their lives. Many individuals unable to cope with this loss have let themselves open to various addictions and underhanded dealings to compensate for this need to be in the limelight.

If it truly is a professional playing career that you feel you are destined to aspire to, then by all means pursue it with the highest of intensity and give it your best shot. Keep in mind that this dream, even if attained, will definitely end. Hopefully when this day arrives you will have already prepared a plan of action in realizing your personal and professional goals which represent the remainder of your life.

CHAPTER 11

HOW TO CHOOSE THE CAREER THAT'S RIGHT FOR YOU

How often do you see people who have been working many years at the same position and simply dread going to their jobs in the morning? Better yet, think of the individuals you know who have spent years of educational training and post-graduate work only to find out shortly after accepting positions that they are in the wrong field or are in a career that was nothing like they thought it would be.

Unfortunately, one of the main concerns of industry today is that too many people are in jobs that are not suited for them. The result is a lot of discontented employees who become less productive with lower initiative and self-esteem Studies have shown that nearly 50% of the American workforce in the 70s were dissatisfied with their jobs. With the advent of automation and a more demanding economy, people are now finding themselves either without jobs or in positions unrelated to their field of study. But making a career change can be difficult especially for individuals who either have too many responsibilities to risk a career change, are not qualified, or are too old to become retrained in a career that they truly desire.

The intent of this chapter is to present guidelines to help you avoid falling into the same dilemma by giving you insight in choosing and developing a career that's right for you.

When developing your career, an approach to use in discovering areas of interest is to determine what activity you would pursue for pure enjoyment and satisfaction had you the entire day to spend with all your financial needs taken care of. This may sound somewhat idealistic, but remember, we're talking about how you plan to dedicate anywhere from ⅓ to ½ of each working day for the remainder of your life.

By buying this publication, many of you have already made that career decision and may be in a position to make the necessary moves. However, before you give that final commitment and pick up the stakes, let's make sure the world of sports has as much to offer you as you think it does. As has already beenstated, disillusionment of a particular field has crushed many a dream and left numerous turnover victims searching for the right fit in the marketplace.

If the approach was taken of pursuing a career as an ideal way to spend each day much like a hobby or side activity, a great deal of the sports enthusiasts would likely choose to be a professional athlete of some sort. Obviously, most of us would fall short of realizing this goal due to physical limitations and formal training. For many who may or may not have an athletic background, just being around the atmosphere and environment where the action takes place can be a fulfilling occupation since sports is the love of their life. Yet we also see professionals, such as athletes, who are unable to accept positions in their respective areas after retirement because they are no longer on top directly doing it.

How then do we develop a plan for the career that includes both the ideal lifestyle and yet can still be realistically attainable? What it boils down to is where are "your" priorities regard-

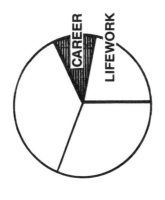

SELF GOALS

LIFEWORK GOALS

RELATIONSHIP GOALS

FIG 1

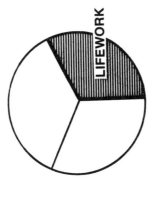

LIFEWORK

FIG 2

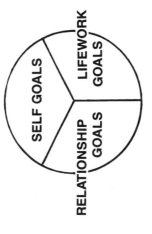

CAREER

LIFEWORK

FIG 3

ing salary, travel, self-esteem, personal investment, etc., that you are willing to accept and sacrifice in both your own and, if applicable, your family's situation?

First, let's examine some simple definitions and concepts that may shed some light in providing direction in the career development process.

Before one may even consider any particular career or vocation, development of life planning goals should be formulated. Life planning involves a comprehensive approach aimed at satisfying all areas of a balanced, integrated life style. (See Figure 1) Remember that if any one of these life style goals suffers a breakdown or has its needs unfulfilled, the frustration and dissatisfaction that results will cause inner turmoil and unrest to the individual and those around him/her no matter how well the other goals or areas are sufficed. The higher the emphasis or priority placed upon an unmet goal, the greater the frustration that will persist.

This is why ideally it is most advantageous to soul search and develop career goals in one's early 20s when time constraints, responsibilities, and financial commitments are usually somewhat minimal. The situation of the aspiring student is reverse in terms to the position of the individual who is in a midlife pattern seeking a career change and has various binding commitments which will affect any decision made. If a career decision is made without taking these other aspects into consideration, and even though the choice appears appropriate, it very well could cause a disruption in other life planning goals (i.e. those involving the family).

Take for example a father who takes a career changing position as a sports administrator in southern Florida. Though "he" couldn't be happier his wife and family may be disenchanted since they despise the heat and find humid summers very unhealthy. Adding fuel to the problem they have now moved away from cherished relatives and friends besides taking a huge loss in the selling of their home. What appears to be an excellent career move turns out only to be a disaster in the life planning process.

The greater the number of liabilities that are acquired as one either experiences bad luck or becomes older, the more difficult it becomes to integrate newly found career and lifestyle goals. As has been already stated, individuals who are unhappy with their present positions or careers many times will not pursue new interests due to the fear of taking risks, a lack of adequate education or training, accelerated age, or a structured environment as such that does not allow for the time and financial independence required to start a new career. What is being said here is not that once a certain age is attained that career development becomes cemented and stagnant, but that to make career changes and pursue new paths could, depending on the individual's situation, present obstacles and barriers which will require additional self-discipline and numerous sacrifices to overcome. This is not to say that making a career change or a position enhancement "within" a career is difficult, but on the contrary, may be more effective and probable during midlife since an individual has already established himself and has attained promotable skills. Never underestimate the value of experience or practical knowledge!

In a later chapter it will be explained on how to convert existing education and expertise into a sports position or career that "appears" not to have similar qualifications.

It is the strong opinion of this author that individuals need to diversify their educational experience and acquire "any" practical experience that will later provide a variety of career alternatives. Early completion of a college degree or certificate is not as important as making sure that the training is applicable and geared towards your occupational goals. Therefore, take time off to explore various fields and discover your self-interests keeping in mind that the main reasons cited by individuals seeking career changes were because "the chosen field was nothing like I thought it would be" or "the course work at school was not indicative of how I would spend my career lifestyle." Many industrial psychologists believe a major fault in the educational system has been its inability to present students with realistic views of what to expect and be prepared for in the work force. In their defense, educational administrators believe their role is to educate the total person not to provide knowledge just for the sake of acquiring a job.

Considering ⅓ of a balanced lifestyle is devoted to the use of an individual's potential in a work setting, (see Figure 2) a broader definition of work needs to be understood. The term "work" encompasses employment that may be of a noncompensatory nature involving volunteer positions, avocations, child rearing, etc., as well as the typical paid employment, which may be classified as either job or career oriented.

To differentiate between the two, those who desire a more structured day, guaranteed salary, security, and stable benefits without as much position diversity or mobility, would probably fall into the work definition of a basic job. This category is paid by the hour and involves such sports positions as the office support staff, equipment managers, maintenance crews, and the stadium groundskeepers. Qualifications in this area are minimal with most skills attained on the job.

If an individual is seeking self-fulfillment, a flexible workday, a compensation structure that rewards creativity, demanding challenges, and opportunities for mobility, then this person would be considered career oriented. These positions are classified as company or monthly salaried and due to their more technical nature, require a great deal more experience and training.

Career-minded individuals many times have a wider range of choices when changing fields and since many of the skills and experiences they acquired are interchangeable with other professions, the transition to another endeavor can be smoother.

It should become more and more clear that career development evolves around the foundation of "knowing thyself" and discovering the many personal activities that lead to a work identity. (See Figure 3). This process implies a conscious and continued growth which leads to the expansion of applicable skills and the knowledge acquired through various learning experiences.

To further assist individuals in forming a system of life style and career goals, Maslow's "hierarchy of needs" may be instituted to establish priorities for future decisions.

According to Abraham Maslow, a psychologist specializing in motivation, unsatisfied needs serve as primary motivators and it is the priority of meeting these needs which will influence behavior and dictate how we may approach a life style plan.

The pyramid approach seen in Figure 4 illustrates a stepping stone format whereby the lowest level of need must be met or satisfied before proceeding to attain the next level of priority.

The most basic needs involve those of a physiological nature including food, shelter, and sex. Without these it would be impossible to seek existence. Safety and security represent those physical or emotional aspects including family and relationship ties which allow for one's daily comfort zone. Following this system of prioritized needs are those of social recognition and self-esteem. Whereby self-esteem establishes a state of confidence and feeling good about oneself's identity, social recognition perpetuates an image of prestige and public awareness in the individual's community. Self-actualization completes the pyramid and is considered to be the ultimate goal in acquiring personal satisfaction. By creating a life style that involves an independence to design, develop, and dictate one's personal career status quo, self-actualization unfortunately, will probably never be realistically accomplished by many.

It should be pointed out that even though Maslow has defined a proven model it is the author's belief in order to be successful, that the level of needs must be individually established and prioritized for each person. The various levels may differ from individual to individual as also

Figure 4

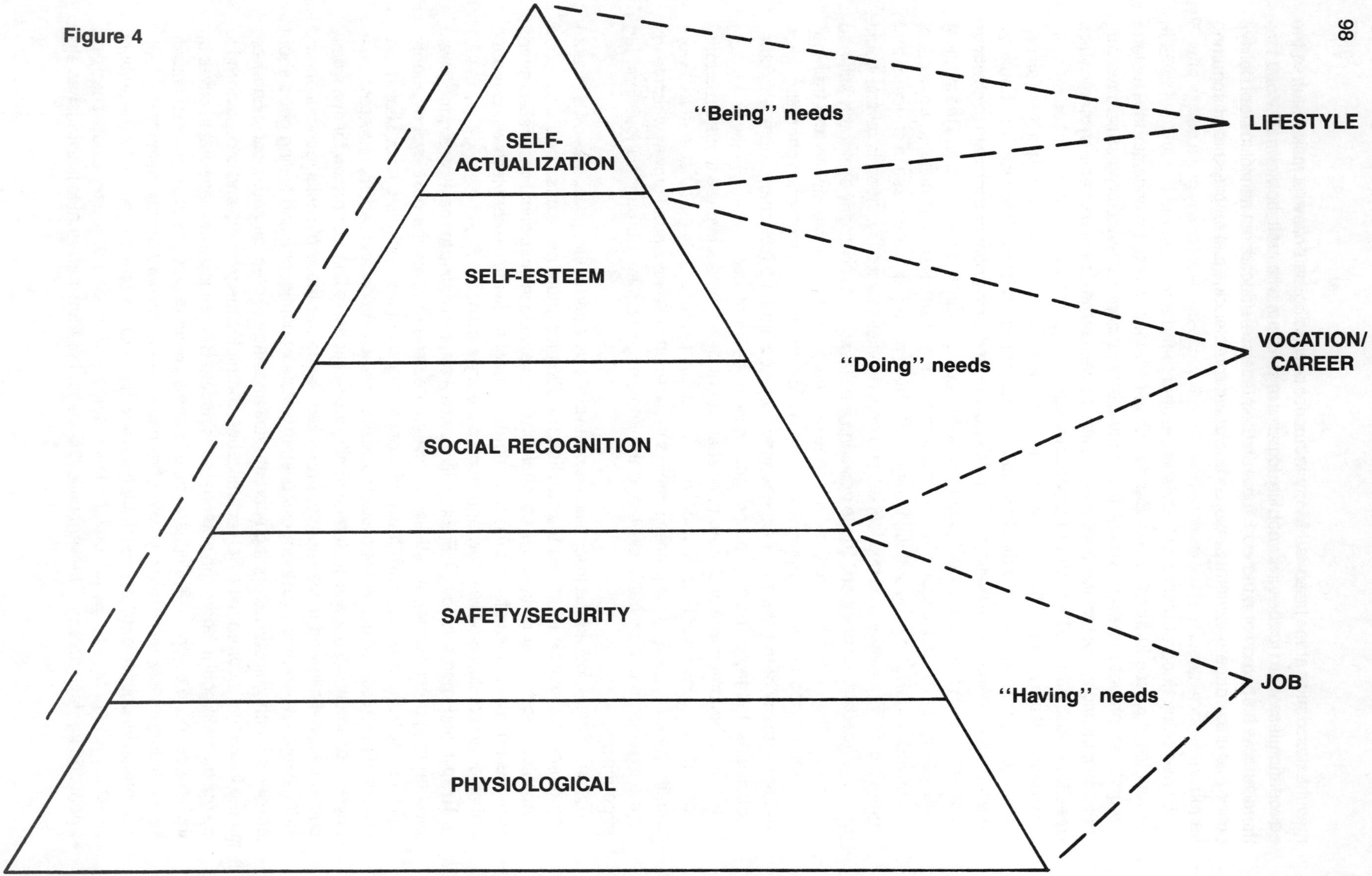

LIFESTYLE

VOCATION/CAREER

JOB

"Being" needs

"Doing" needs

"Having" needs

SELF-ACTUALIZATION

SELF-ESTEEM

SOCIAL RECOGNITION

SAFETY/SECURITY

PHYSIOLOGICAL

may the description of the need itself. For instance, many individuals have replaced a perceived meaningless need in their life such as social recognition with a more appropriate need for them such as belonging or attachment. Many may also find self-actualization not to be suitably defined and therefore reterm that level as social independence. To exemplify this point even further, those individuals who are workaholics and are success oriented may place next in priority to their basic need of physiological needs, self-actualization.

Fitting existing models or theories to meet an individual's life style plan is not the goal in career development. What is important is forming a hierarchy or system of goals that will be both practical and consistent with today's needs and business environment, while still providing satisfaction and guidelines which will allow for smooth personal and career transitions in the years to come.

For those who wish to seek a career development pattern which illustrates the various age stages in a life-work cycle, Super, a well known industrial psychologist, has developed the following model:

AGE	STAGE	DEVELOPMENT
014	GROWTH	Physical; Social; Mental
15-25	EXPLORATORY	Soul Searching; Choices based on education and practical experience
26-45	ESTABLISHMENT	Career meshed; creation of a work identity
45-65	MAINTENANCE	Status quo; financial and career security
65-	DECLINE	Exit from work force; increased delegation of responsibilities

Since most individuals possibly will vary their development within each stage due to such factors as the timeliness of a new career or the severity of obstacles that may be encountered at the time, this model should therefore be viewed as a guideline that represents the general work-life cycle of those who were successful in establishing long standing careers without many career or job changes. Many industrial psychologists have concluded that considering the amount of sacrifices, the paying of dues, and the time it takes to create an identity in the work force, a per son must weather the first ten years of working life as being somewhat underpaid in relation to his/her efforts, while the last 10 years of one's employable lifetime are in comparison overly compensated. In a sense, the decline period in the work cycle financially rewards individuals for the contributions they provided over a professional lifetime.

The life planning process is not intended to push an individual into any one career, rather it is designed to develop well-thought-out decisions that will provide continued satisfaction of life style and career needs as interests and new demands change in the years to come. It is impossible to match characteristics of people to the traits of jobs and still remain all consuming in the long range affect. Both people and careers are dynamic and change overtime. Therefore, individuals must be prepared not only to meet their needs and challenges of today, but also to adapt and accept the demands of the future.

CHAPTER 12

PLAN OF ACTION TO SUCCESS

Even if you know you are qualified and would enjoy a particular position that would be fulfilling today, would you really want to continue that routine for the next 20 years? Better yet, will the pros and cons of your lifestyle inventory be the same in the 1990s as it was in the 1980s? This is a problem for those in the work force who have dead-end positions and are simply looking for new positions.

A good example of this are the coaches in both the college and high school ranks who have little training outside their athletic endeavors and now due to budget cutbacks, age, or changing curriculums, have few employment alternatives. With a limited educational background, there is not much opportunity for upward mobility or job enhancement which is why so many coaches and physical educators are going back to school to diversify their background for future career options.

A trap many aspiring people fall into is becoming lost in the organizational maze which can result in being overlooked for promotions. As a result they're overlooked for promotions through no fault of their own.

Whenever one considers making a career change or going back for retraining, the timing of the move is a key factor. The first step you should take is to develop a time table and to take stock in yourself for a sense of direction to help you reach your ultimate position.

The basic strategy most career developers lack is a "plan of action." To be successful today in athletics, one must be able to look beyond the 1980s to see the needs and the issues of the future. In the last ten years alone there have been more controversial issues and changes in both the collegiate and professional ranks than there have been in the last 50 years. Those in athletics who have sacrificed and prepared themselves to meet future challenges, are the ones who will capitalize on the opportunities and benefits of tomorrow.

There is no better illustration of this than those who are involved in sports medicine, strength coaching, and sports psychology. Not long ago these fields were virtually unheard of, but for the individuals who foresaw their necessity and struggled with the developing stages are now the leaders who are reaping the rewards of their efforts.

Al Davis of the Oakland/Los Angeles Raiders of the NFL, epitomizes a man who looked into the future and developed his thoughts of what he felt was needed for the betterment of professional football. From his involvement with the infant AFL in the early 60s, to his recent franchise move from Oakland to Los Angeles for its enormous television marketing potential, controversial Al Davis realized his dreams despite much pessimism and many hurdles to conquer.

Analyze any great athlete or businessperson and you will realize that talent alone did not breed their success, but it also was the follow through of their plan of action and self-direction that led to the fulfillment of their goals.

Setting Goals in Career Development

Before you can put a plan of action into effect, goals must be established to efficiently channel your energy and effort. The first phase in goal setting is to identify the areas of life in which you have the greatest need to excel for accomplishment. These can be either personal, career-oriented, or even related to your amateur hobbies or sports. In other words, the greater the desire to achieve, the more you will be driven.

In developing your overall career goal to succeed, refer back to your personal inventory and the targeted area of sports you have chosen. With this in mind, try to project in time segments of 1, 5, and 10 years what position or level in your field you would like to be, your most important achievements and personal experiences you acquired, and the responsibilities you would like to be involved in with your social affiliations and family.

Don't forget to include the goals and desires of your spouse and family. Many broken homes today were caused by the lack of communication between spouses in the planning of their careers. Your ten year projection will not be considered a success if only your career goals were satisfied and not your personal and family ones as well.

Hopefully you now have established some definite goals which represent a composite view of your expectations for the future, but do the features and qualities of this projected lifestyle coincide with the information collected from your personal inventory? Rephrased, is there a realistic and feasible transition from your present situation considering strengths and weaknesses, as compared to what it will take for you to attain your future goals?

To be more comfortable with the answers to these questions and confident that you can go from today's dreams to tomorrow's realities, try to identify areas in which you need skill development and a plan of action for improvement. In this plan determine your priorities by determining your willingness to make the necessary sacrifices such as retraining, relocation to another state, personal improvement, etc., in order to accomplish these goals. If you are still in school or have the opportunity to continue your education, make sure you have prepared your training schedule with built-in flexibility for future positions and possible career changes. By concentrating in only one area of study and not having a very diverse program, you are limiting your options and marketability for the future.

Goals need to be as specific as possible. When crystallizing your thinking, keep the following suggestions in mind:

- Open your thinking. Don't assume what you can or can't do without allowing yourself to want it. Being realistic about your background doesn't mean limiting and holding yourself back from a position you want. Be creative and expand your horizons to the limit of your potential.
- Make your goals tangible and measurable. Intangible goals can't be measured and therefore are very difficult in gauging your success. Just stating the conditions that you want an education in sports is an intangible objective. Explicitly stating that you want a Masters degree in Sports Administration by 1989 makes this condition both tangible and measurable.
- The more defined and specific a goal becomes, the easier it will be to visualize and achieve. A good way to separate your goal is to identify between short range (immediate to one year) and long range (one year and beyond) objectives. Your ten-year projections represent your long range goals and therefore will not be as detailed as your immediate short range targets of today.
- Learn to goal balance when conflicts arise between two things you want at the same time, especially when both of these have an equal amount of desire attached to them.

    From time to time as your priorities and values change, you will be confronted with this conflict. Try to determine what benefits will be gained versus the possible loss and risk of each.

Take for example if you have saved money for a trip to Europe and your tuition for the upcoming school year but realistically cannot afford both if you also desire to attend a specialized sports science program that will incur additional costs. The benefits are obvious for each option, but the real difference is seen when comparing the loss of not attending a specialized school which can serve a more long term fulfilling need than either a three week trip or completing your education at a local institution that isn't as well known or does not have as technical of a sports program.

Not all of us would make the same decision in the above example, but once again, priorities and values will differ between individuals and tend to fluctuate through one's life depending on the particular situation.

When a degree of dissonance and uncertainty appears to disrupt life style planning or the prioritizing of goals, a decision will have to be made to determine what will provide the most appropriate and continued satisfaction. Like any decision in life that will eventually be encountered, the following decision making steps will provide direction in formulating a conclusion:

1 - Define the problem or situation
2 - Propose the options and alternatives
3 - Gather information on the options
4 - Evaluate the options

Once a decision has been made, the next step in the process is to act upon the choice. Since the establishment of goals is an integrated part of the decision-making process, the format listed below should be reviewed and employed:

5 - Set goals
6 - Establish a plan of action
7 - Designate target dates
8 - Evaluate, balance, and continually reassess goals making any changes deemed necessary

- Overcome your obstacles and develop confidence in your abilities. Each step in your building block process of accomplishing goals will often present an additional obstacle that could stand in the way of future goals. Don't go around these obstacles by finding solutions and setting goals that are easily attained causing you not to be challenged and motivated. At the same time if your obstacles do not have a viable solution, then possibly the goals are too high and need to be reevaluated through your personal inventory.

Now you are ready to begin pursuing what could very well be one of the most important developmental periods of your life. Though at times it may appear to that you may be falling away from your goals, the only way you can gauge your progress is to monitor and chart your actions with your written plan of action.

THE DREAM CAREER MODEL — TAKING STOCK IN YOURSELF

Since many of you have already decided to pursue a career in the world of sports, the next step is to determine what personal strengths and weaknesses you presently possess so that you may be able to narrow down your choices and gauge your market value. One means of assessing your interests and potential is by taking personality profiles and general aptitude surveys. These can be administered by either your high school counselor, college relations office, the human resource division with your employer, or possibly the psychological measurement bureau in any university psychology department. Results can be interpreted by a professional who can point out interests and qualities that you may never have realized existed.

A model in career planning and lifestyle management developed by the author utilizes the principle of fantasizing (Figure 5). This process of finding a dream position starts with the premise that if an individual had all financial, family, and personal responsibilities taken care of, how then would he/she spend each day and still remain motivated and self-actualizing? Some individuals have indicated that since they would no longer have a care in the world, spending their time on a beach would be quite a life. But after a few months, beachcombing could become somewhat old and not very personally satisfying for the next few years.

Enthusiasts with sports crazed personalities targeted professional playing careers as their fantasy walk of life. Once again, would a professional playing career be all that attractive if we knew how each day was really spent? Better yet, you may say that playing professionally "is" your dream, but you may lack either the physical attributes or playing experience needed to accomplish this feat. Where then, you may wonder, does fantasizing become an asset rather than a drawback?

If you notice in the model, the fantasy career is in a large circle. The reason for this is that even though the chosen fantasy may not always be realistically attainable, there must be some features or qualities about that dream that make it attractive which could still be applicable to another position. Therefore, the goal is not always to attain the fantasy itself, but to develop a career that is somewhat "around" or represented by similar job descriptions and characteristics. Since it has been discovered that people are more productive and healthier in work they enjoy doing, it becomes paramount that individuals dream, fantasize, or envision themselves in occupations performing roles and tasks similar to those associated with interests that excite them in their personal ventures, hobbies, or recreational activities.

This model allows room for individual differences because not everyone would choose a hobby or personal interest that they enjoy for a career. This is why an earlier chapter in establishing a priority of needs and goal setting will provide the necessary direction needed in the fantasy-career process. Even though an individual may enjoy sports as a recreational activity, it may not provide the financial benefits or job security that another field may offer. Another hidden drawback for those in the work force who have pursued careers identifiable with their hobbies and leisure activities is that they may no longer experience the emotional release or enjoyment they once cherished in their participation. The daily presssure of providing results and balancing budgets may reduce the interest of making personal interests a viable career.

It cannot be overemphasized the need to be creative and imaginative in allowing your mind to flow, no matter what the idea. Many a successful career has started from a whim that was either considered not practical or too risky. It is never too early to begin career development considering that successful occupational planning is nothingmore than the culmination of implementing personal experiences and interests. If you find that discovering your fantasy career does not come very easily, leave the circle empty and proceed onward to the next phase which will hi-lite personal characteristics and preferences. After completing the various steps of the model, along with the usage of other interest tools, it may become more evident the type of career that should be pursued taking into account your personal inventory.

Taking Stock in Yourself

When taking stock in yourself, list all your natural and developed strengths which you feel could be an asset and marketed in your job campaign. At the same time identify all your known deficiencies and areas where you are weak and lacking development.

Possible strengths could be an individual's ability to work under pressure, developed journalistic and writing talents, self-discipline, good communication skills, and an outgoing personality. Possible weaknesses could include an individual's lack of aggressiveness, emotional instability, an inability to work well with numbers, or a poor speaking voice in front of an audience.

It should be pointed out that items categorized as strengths and weaknesses are not consistently defined the same way by all. What one individual may feel is a strength in his/her life may very well be a weakness for another or possibly conceived as neither a strength or a weakness. For instance, some may view family support, financial assets, and close personal ties as a definite strength while others may neither possess these aspects or find them necessary in life-style or career planning. It becomes apparent that there is a need for soul searching and self-evaluating oneself objectively in order to paint a clear and concise career picture.

Several sessions should be taken at this task with the inventory ideally being completed in several sittings. It is better to write down a few ideas and come back to the brainstorm process from time to time. Try to jot down thoughts as you think of them or as characteristics are pointed out to you by others. Continue to update and add to this list, preferably 15-25 items, until you have exhausted the ability to recognize traits and factors that are pertinent in your lifestyle.

What is even more imperative here is the prioritizing of items in each category from the one's with the greatest value to those of the lowest value. In other words it is important to realize which strengths are most outstanding and need to be emphasized in career planning as well as defining the weaknesses which will or will not present the biggest shortcomings. Remember that a weakness or insufficiency has the ability to later become a strength or not as dominant of a weakness "if" you are able to retrain, compensate, or develop the trait in question. This 'if' has been the singlemost difference between those who make it happen and those who watch it happen in the marketplace.

By taking stock of your physical and intellectual qualities, you may be able to match your assets with the many job descriptions as well as discover areas that need improvement. If your goal is to become a public relations director for a NFL franchise and you don't possess good speaking qualiites and writing skills, then obviously you must improve these areas or choose a position that is more conducive to your talents. Remember too if you didn't have the potential or the desire to improve on a skill that is lacking or undeveloped then you should move on to an area where you are not only more qualified, but also where you are more willing to make the necessary sacrifice to improve these deficiencies.

Once you are comfortable with this inventory, begin another list of the pros and cons in what you consider to be essential in your ideal work day. Pros, could be considered the daily aspects which of are high importance to you, and the cons, represent features that you wouldn't especially like to have as part of your day. Once again it is necessary to prioritize to the order from the most to the least important items in each category. No matter what career you choose to eventually pursue, it will undoubtedly have a certain amount of meaningful and undesirable traits. Since there exists no utopia or flawless decision, it is preferable to look upon a choice as a matter of what is better for the situation instead of viewing it as right or wrong. By goal balancing and assessing a needs clarification, you will be better equipped to determine what points are of the utmost value and therefore should be satisfied first and what negative qualities or undesirable features are the most or least likely to be tolerated. This model therefore serves more than a tool in career development, but may be utilized at any time in life planning management.

Some comparisons that you will likely make, and even some that may appear right now to be of no concern but very well could be in the years ahead, are listed below in the categories

Figure 5

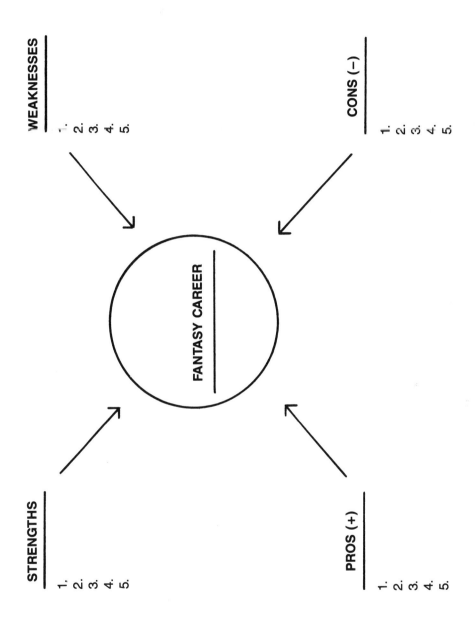

of lifework values, relationship values, and personal values. If you are going to utilize these values in your personal inventory, attach a level of importance to each item to clarify their degree of need. Again, no one category is more important than the other since if the needs in one area are not sufficed or met, the disharmony of not fulfilling priorities will result in dissatisfaction through the entire life planning system.

1. *Lifework Values*

   Chance for career development and advancement; increased responsibilities
   Opportunity for mental challenge, stimulation and intellectual growth
   Opportunity to persuade, motivate, teach others
   Opportunity to serve others; address a social issue or concern
   Adequate reimbursement for work done; pay equal to contribution
   Flexible hours or part-time work commitment
   Ability to move around physically from place to place; mobility; travel; relocation
   Job security
   Minimal stress and pressure in a work situation
   Evenings and weekends free from work-related duties
   Time and energy for my "other" life
   Physical work
   Satisfying, meaningful work that seems important
   Work with people
   Minimal people contact; work alone
   Desire to work with numbers, data, machines, objects
   Be part of a team; work cooperatively with a group of equals
   Supportive work relationship with co-workers and colleagues
   Work that uses my skills, knowledge, and abilities to the fullest
   Chance to see results; have a tangible product
   Recognition for achievements; status, prestige
   Chance to use own ideas; be creative
   Opportunity to control own work; make own decisions; be own boss
   Have well-defined, routine responsibilities; clear supervision
   Chance for personal growth and development on the job
   Commission; incentive salary; guaranteed income

2. *Relationship Values*

   Open honest communications
   Knowing I am needed by significant others
   A strong, healthy family life
   Availability to meet needs of children, partner, relatives, friends
   Free of permanent attachments to others
   Having a large circle of friends, acquaintances
   In-depth friendships; one or two close personal friends
   Access to a circle of supportive, accepting relationships
   Contact with challenging people — people from whom I can learn
   Acquaintances, friendships from many backgrounds, ages
   Close friendships with the same sex (opposite sex)
   Compatible co-workers and colleagues
   A good solid, one-to-one relationship
   Access to people I can help; with whom I feel useful

Friendships with people who share my values, lifestyle, etc.
Ability to deal effectively with conflict, criticism, confrontation
Winning the approval of others
Awareness that relationships are more important than task
Raising healthy, independent children
Being a good partner and/or parent

3. *Personal Values*
Feelings of self-esteem; self-confidence
Ability to meet my own needs; assertiveness
Being in control of my life; feeling responsible for my behavior
Knowing that I am liked by other persons; winning the approval of others
Freedom from anxiety, pressure, stress
Time and space for myself
An inner sense of serenity; at peace with self
A desire for independence
Experiencing a sense of personal accomplishment; feeling productive
Ability to cope with whatever comes; flexibility; adaptability
Opportunities for leisure time; ability to have fun
Financial security
Ability to express and manage emotions
Feeling physically fit and healthy
A spiritual dimension in life; a set of religious or ethical beliefs
Intellectual growth and stimulation; opportunity to learn
Freedom from dependencies on alcohol, drugs, overeating, relationships
Respect for good use of time and energy
Willingness to take risks; enjoy adventure
A competitive spirit; enjoy "winning"
Need for stability, security, and a degree of certainty
A well-groomed personal appearance
A comfortable home; a personal retreat
Need for healthy sexual expression

4. *Intangible Values and Practical Needs*
Weather conditions; climate
Local entertainment; cultural status
Work location (urban, suburban, rural)
Transportation (public, private, carpool); traffic; distance to commute
Day care arrangements
Travel opportunities
Benefits (health insurance, life insurance, sick leave, vacation)
Cost of living indexes
Housing and living quarters
Wardrobe (casual, professional, uniform)
Conservatively managed firm (liberal)
Recreation opportunities
Major communication center (airport, railway)

This is just a sample of the many factors that will influence your lifestyle. Chances are that the list you develop will change through the course of your life as you reevaluate personal values. Continuously update your priorities so that you are always aware of what you expect from your employment. One of the keys to job satisfaction is making sure that the qualities which motivate you and are most meaningful to you are present in your work environment.

With this composite picture of your strengths, values and preferences, it's time to start looking at specific areas of sports and narrowing them down to the position that's right for you.

CHAPTER 13

ORGANIZATIONAL QUALITIES

If coaches care to employ a staff under their control, then they must be a good administrator and organizer. Coaches become the overseers of all that happens with their assistants and players. Many coaches prefer to play an active role in only a few components of the "big picture" to the total operation. They are primarily the decision-makers concurring in player positions, practice schedules, game plans, trades, and other organizational moves.

In governing the energies of all involved toward a common purpose, coaches will be required to delegate duties and place trust in those assigned to the tasks. For some first time head coaches, the transition of taking upon the total spectrum of duties as opposed to performing one specialty as an assistant becomes overbearing. Some coaches prefer to remain in an assistant's capacity since they do not feel comfortable on the larger more involved level.

The trademark of the great coaches was their meticulous organization of time and people's energies. So often it is seen where championship calibre teams will spend the least amount of time in training camps as well as having practice sessions that last no longer than 90 minutes. These same organized and to the point coaches are characterized by having time to themselves and outlet activities as opposed to the workaholic type who has 2-3 hour practice sessions and who spends nights sleeping in their offices watching reels of film right up to game day.

A major drawback to this all-consuming approach is the high incidence of burnout among players and coaches alike. It is many times reflected in the performance of play especially late in the season. Knowing how to win is one thing, being able to get a team to peak is another.

The Need to be Flexible

Few coaches retire or quit coaching by choice. Success is short lived, and for those unable to adapt and move on to another page in the journey of success, it can be even shorter. Many coaches are forced to exit the ranks because they are unable to move with the times or simply lose touch with realizing that what was good for yesterday may not be so good for today. As far as dealing with the social trends and fads of players, Bud Grant, ex-coach of the Minnesota Vikings, said it best: "We may not always agree with the signs of the times, but we must find a way to effectively work within its framework."

Coaches who have left their mark on a sport can be best seen as instigators of change, not reactors. Unfortunately coaches as a whole are not great innovators and can be characterized as a collection of copycats willing to jump on the bandwagon of something that has proven to be successful. The pioneer coach seems to always be ahead of his peers who are merely trying to keep status quo. There also seems to be one distinct advantage to being a successful trendsetter — job security.

Another major mistake many tunnel-visioned coaches encounter is not allowing the personnel make-up of the team dictate the type of play or strategy to be employed. Rigid thinking here can only lead to under utilized talent and a possible job firing.

Not only should a chemistry exist between the style of play withthe team's personality, but also between the head coach and the organization's management regarding its commitment to winning. Too often in their great desire to land a head coach's position, people will take the job without ever looking into the past history of why others left the team. A new coach should make sure that a marriage exists with the organization guaranteeing that the employer's commitments and philosophies are the same as his/her's. If not, it is better to wait for another opportunity to arrive to establish oneself's credibility in a workable environment.

This situation is common in the collegiate ranks especially with struggling programs. The schools themselves play musical chairs when establishing goals and priorities. At one point the institution may provide lip service that education is of a main focal point only to come back later when ticket sales are down due to losing and bend the rules to NCAA regulations to preserve an entertainment commodity. If a coach is to function properly, then there can be no inconsistencies in the expectations of what he/she is to deliver. It usually is one of the incongruent program priorities that is laid upon a coach when deciding to terminate his contract. What he/she was giving full reign to do upon being hired is now the means to dismissal.

Secondary Schools

The majority of all salaried coaches will be employed by secondary school districts. Unlike the professional circle where winning at all costs and securing a profit are the goals of that entertainment industry, high school coaches are hired as educators to teach student-athletes about sports and life. Many coaches lose sight of this fact and subsequently get caught up in their own egotistical ideals or the concept of professionalism.

In developmental terms, the school coach is probably the most important member of all coaching ranks. This becomes apparent when considering that he/she can turn a student on to further sports competition or possibly make the experience so negative that the child may begin to dislike sports and fitness of any form. There would be no future college or professional performer if the school coach does not take his/her responsibility of forming a foundation to life for his/her players seriously.

For a number of students the coach becomes a substitute parent or fills a void in the personal life of the child. Coaches in these situations rarely need to put themselves in a position of high authority because the child has already placed them on a pedestal as such. So many coaches get caught up in the mechanical side of sport that they become blinded to adolescent needs and concerns. Few students ever forget their coaches and the impact they had on their lives.

Secondary school coaches, however, can not relegate their involvement to the gym or field alone. They must ultimately work effectively with parents, booster groups, school principals and athletic directors, and even with the communities' political structure which adopts guidelines for athletic participation. The area of controversy that will take the most tact in handling will be with those who want to win at any price or parents who feel their children are not receiving a fair shake. A coach must have the moral courage as well as the backing of the school's administration to stand his/her ground when he/she truly believes that he/she is doing the correct thing.

When establishing a system of priorities, a coach must understand that academics come first and family activities second. Since a word from the coach, particularly if that person is a strong role model, often has more impact than that from a parent, coaches should be cognizant of the effect any statement they may make to students, especially if it is not consistent with the family's or school's philosophy towards discipline and education.

A common concern expressed by many student-athletes and parents is that coaches are not open to working with players with varying degrees of talent. It is easy to develop the highly skilled performer, but again, participation and enjoyment should be the main thrust at this level. For the less talented young person, this may be the only opportunity to achieve a sense of accomplishment in what probably will be a one-time involvement in team sports.

Not only does this "teacher of sport" need to be proficient at demonstrating physical skills, but must also be even more so adept at creating high sportsmanship ideals. Sports psychologists believe that sports is becoming more conducive to building "characters" rather than character as once perceived. Meshing high standards and values along with teaching the physical game makes this sometimes thankless part-time position a near full-time preoccupation.

Those wishing to secure a coaching role will find jobs tougher to find with declining enrollments and subsequent school closings. There also is a considerable turnover at this level with coaches moving on to college sports or other careers due to the low pay of the teaching and coaching profession. Varsity positions are also tougher to find since the pay scale is higher and many of them are occupied by teachers with numerous years of experience who also have their pension tied in with their extracurricular activities. However, with the onset of Title IX, there has never been a sufficient number of female coaches to fill the demand which many counterparts have reluctantly taken. Vacancies are also more prevalent in the urban areas as opposed to suburban school districts largely in part so because the inner city students take on part-time jobs at an earlier age thus keeping participation numbers down. Coaching in the city has become more challenging considering that the instructor must both motivate and many times solicit students to become involved.

Salaries vary upon each community's emphasis on sport, but the average scale would be $2500.00-$3000.00 for a varsity position with assistants receiving in the neighborhood of $1500.00. Some school districts even have a sliding scale for longer season sports or for those which are non-revenue producers.

You should be aware that each state has its own requirements for physical educators, teachers and coaches. Keep your eye posted on job advertisements inthe spring of the year or call the local school district on hiring procedures.

College Coaching

The collegiate scene presents a completely different picture to coaching from that experienced at the high school ranks. With a much more highly skilled and talented athlete to work with, teaching will become more highly technical and specialized. The environment from which a coach will operate will be better equipped and considerably more prestigious. This highly desired level of coaching has considerable benefits to be gained which will not easily be attained without a price to be paid.

Coaches aspiring to become a part of a collegiate program should do so as soon as possible since it becomes much more difficult to enter this level if one has been entrenched in the secondary school format. The most direct route is to apply as an assistant at a Division II or III program or enter a Division I school by means as a graduate assistant. Most graduate assistantships do not offer a salary in compliance with NCAA regulations, but what will be provided is room and board and even more importantly, a chance to have a "foot in the door" at an early age.

A small percentage of college coaching is spent on the practice field and can more or less be viewed as a position divided into ⅓'s. For a head coach, ⅓ of his time will be spent coaching the physical game, ⅓ administrative and organization duties, and ⅓ recruiting. During the off-season months, his coaching segment is replaced by the now all important function of fund-raising and for some smaller schools, this may be a year round adventure.

Full-time assistants can expect to spend days and weeks on the road recruiting potential athletes. This is the aspect of collegiate coaching that few coaches enjoy since it does seem to take them on every lonely highway forcing them to be away from their families. For this very reason alone, many individuals leave the ranks since the divorce rate, like any other "on the road" profession, is very high for coaches.

Recruiting is a difficult task that cannot be learned overnight and is an element of collegiate sports that is tough to master for any high school coach, no matter how successful he/she has been. Just ask Jerry Faust, ex-coach of Notre Dame's football program, who only lost a handful of games in 17 years as a high school coach, but didn't even have a .500 record as a collegiate mentor.

The younger coaches or graduate assistants can expect to perform a myriad of tasks from splicing game films by position to recruiting athletes in virtually unknown locations. Rarely will persons serving in these capacities spend more than 2-3 years at any given institution.

Every would-be college coach should fully acquaint himself/herself with scholarship rules and recruiting regulations provided by the NCAA.

Salaries in the collegiate circles will vary upon the size of school and the conference they compete in. Assistants usually begin in the range of $20,000-30,000 with Division II and III schools paying less. Head coaches can expect compensation for men's sports starting at $35,000 to $50,000 while female mentors will receive less. Major conference head coaches in revenue sports can realize 6-digit salary figures not counting their outside income derived from radio and television shows, sports summer camps, endorsements, and speaking engagements.

Professional Sports

The professional arena is the only "pure" arena for an individual who wants to simply coach and nothing else. Pro coaches need not concern themselves with the unique problems experienced by the school programs such as recruiting, counseling, academic eligibility, fundraising, or complying with administrative policies.

In order to secure a professional coaching position, one must first be successful at a lower level. It becomes obvious that the college football and basketball scene is the proving grounds for both its players and coaches. But for baseball and hockey which have a minor league system, a parent franchise may keep a coach under a watchful eye for several years before any permanent decision is made. Amazingly enough, the win-loss records of a minor league coach is not the main criteria for being selected as a head coach, but his ability to teach, develop, and nurture raw talent is.

Never be intimidated by the fact that you may not have played professionally because many of the top coaches in the 4 major sports also never competed professionally.

Salaries for professional coaches are many times twice as high as they are for collegiate assistants and head coaches. The emphasis will be on winning over anything else thus allowing for individuals to establish a reputation quicker than is possible with collegiate sports. As far as job security, it is rare to see a professional coach or assistant remain with one club for more than 5 years. This is so when considering the emphasis on winning and the need to create immediate results as well as the fact that most assistants make continuous moves to better enhance their possibilities of becoming a head coach.

Other Areas of Opportunity

Coaching is by no means restricted to only the schools and professional leagues or even just the 4 major media sports. Opportunities exist in nearly every conceivable sport at private clubs, health centers, or golf and tennis operations. Some of these areas have already been touched upon in the chapter, "Playing Professionally" whereby these sports are governed by national associations.

There are, however, other organizations that provide opportunities to coach. The one major drawback is that since many of these sports are either struggling to create an identity or have limited budgets, the coaching staffs will receive minimal forms of compensation.

The U.S. Olympic Committee recognizes nearly three dozen national sports organizations all in need of dedicated instructors. By obtaining a copy of the USOC's directory, you will be able to obtain contacts in your local area.

Never rule out YMCA's, YWCA's, or the nearest recreation center. These organizations are always in dire need of additional manpower, not to mention that the experience could become invaluable on your resume.

CHAPTER 14

VALIDATING A CAREER CHOICE

The first step in discovering a more precise picture of your chosen career is to call upon someone who is active in the field or participates in the position as a full time employee.

By going out in the trenches you will not only be getting a feel for the position and its consequential typical day, but hopefully you will be exposed to the lifestyle it entices, the personal sacrifices that must be encountered, and the necessary individual traits that will be required to be a true success.

Many times a local professional franchise, collegiate team, athletic organization, or consulting firm will suffice this need. It is better to contact someone you know or set up an appointment with a person who has been referred to you be a close source in an organization. Following this format the informational interview may be more welcomed since such high demands are placed on the time of professionals in the sports world. If you do not have a source or someone that may provide you with a lead, take it upon yourself to make a "cold call."

In the informational interview, be professional and well prepared when stating the nature of your inquiry. Don't be discouraged. Administrators and professionals in athletics are always looking for individuals with firm convictions who are confident and aggressive. If nothing else, they may grant you an interview or at least refer you to someone who may have the time to better serve you.

When I myself sought an athletic internship following completion of my undergraduate studies, I approached a local professional hockey club with an internship proposal. Since I was directed to call upon the president of the organization who handled such matters, it became frustrating of me to never be able to reach him on the telephone. But through my tenacity over a period of time, we eventually, made a connection. Though he didn't have any opportunities available, I was invited to meet with him and present my ideas solely because he was so impressed that a young man could be so persistent and approach him in a very professional manner.

What this is demonstrates is that even though every organization might not be this receptive, there are professional people willing to spend time with individuals who could well be their future employees. You don't have to call on major organizations. Local doctors, high school personnel, collegiate staff members, and voluntary organizations are more accessible, and more likely to put you on a temporary project to give you a better feel for the work that could lead to future considerations.

Once you have chosen a position to be researched and have established a contact for an informational interview, prepare a set of questions that will better able you to discover aspects which you deem important. The Occupational Research Worksheet on the next page provides a guideline or the most pertinent information regarding a new position. Feel free to add or delete targeted skills or values you consider to be a priority in "your" situation.

If you have already chosen a field of endeavor and are now seeking employment, the Job Factors Inventory will allow you to examine and determine if this is the employer in which you want to establish your career. Remember, positions may vary from organization to organization and finding the right setting will contribute to your satisfaction or lack of success. Look at professional athletes. Their positions rarely change from club to club, but by switching to a team with a different style on just by being in a new environment, such moves have either enhanced the performance or extended the playing careers of many players.

Never settle for a career or opportunity just because it seems to be similar to what you want. If necessary, take time off from school or work and discover the route that matches your goals and personal inventory. It's better to be disappointed now from disillusionment rather than spend thousands of dollars in education and countless hours preparing for a position with which you will not be satisfied.

Once again after completing several worksheets, you may have to revert back to your priorities and needs and, if necessary, goal balance if either the career or employer you chose lacks certain criteria. If you haven't completed an occupational worksheet on a position or career you plan to move on, do so even if you researched it several years earlier. People change and so do jobs, therefore, never leave yourself unprepared or assuming you know what to expect.

OCCUPATIONAL RESEARCH WORKSHEET

Career/field investigated: _____

Positions related to career: _____

Sources of information: _____

_____

Type of work involved in this field (tasks, duties):_____

_____

_____

Places and environment where this work is done: _____

_____

Background, qualifications for this work: _____

   Education/training: _____

   Experience: _____

   Skills, personal strengths:_____

_____

Practical factors to consider: _____

_____

   Salary: _____Benefits: _____

   Hours: _____Location: _____

Means to advancement: _____

Special concerns for women: _____

Employment outlook: Current:_____Future:_____

Do your interests, skills, values, and practical needs match this particular work choice: __

Other observations or impressions: _____

JOB FACTORS INVENTORY

I. TASK RELATED
Responsibility — Will there be enough to stimulate you? Too much or too little?
Pressure — High? Variable? Even?
Variety — Are many different tasks required?
Decisions — Will you make any? How important will their input be?
Creativity — Do you have an opportunity to implement your own ideas?
Tangible Product — Is there a concrete product you can point to?
Expertise — Ability to use your special skills/knowledge?

II. ENVIRONMENT RELATED
Salary — Low or high wages? Fixed? Incentive? Commission?
Opportunity — Can you promote easily from this position?
Hours and Time Flexibility — Structured (9-5)? Flexible? More than 40 hours? More than 5 days weekly?
Dress — Casual? Professional? Uniform?
Parking and Transportation — Is parking costly? Free? Is much time spent in transportation to and from work? Are these high traffic routes?
Work Atmosphere — Light enough? Privacy adequate? Pleasant colors? Comfortable furnishings? Comfortable temperature? How noisy? Any windows?
Work Space — Confined? Free to move from area to area?
Travel Opportunities — What percent of work week?

III. RELATIONSHIP RELATED
Supervision — How closely supervised will you be? Does your supervisor appear to be supportive? Helpful? Is the firm conservative or liberally managed?
Status — Is the position one that conveys the respect of others?
Team Work — Do you enjoy working closely with others?
Co-workers — Do they appear friendly? Likeable? Closed? Open?
Service to Others — Do your responsibilities include helping others?

CHAPTER 15

AREAS FOR ACQUIRING EXPERIENCE

In seeking a job in the sports profession, there are two main factors that separate the best candidates from the rest of the pack — experience and contacts. Whether it be volunteer work, internship, or salaried experience, it's never too soon to start acquiring skills and developing contacts for future employment. Due to the large degree of organized athletic activities for nearly every segment of the population, there will be less competition for the positions in the less publicized non-traditional sports like women's basketball and men's softball, than those associated with a major professional organization or franchise. It's not the size of the firm or the sport that will add meaning to your credentials, but rather the quality of the experience you gained which will make you more marketable.

As has already been pointed out, you'll be surprised that with the proper approach how many top sports executives will be receptive to sit down with you to discuss the intricacies of a particular position and possibly even put you on a volunteer project to get your feet wet. By being professional and assertive with your contacts, you'll be making an impression on the team's management, and if the occasion should arise where a vacancy does open, you may be in the right place at the right time to fill that vacancy. Remember that you must be more innovative and aggressive than the next person who's pursuing your same interests if you are to crack into a tough job market.

Some top administrators have entered the field in some novel ways. Take for example this story which was printed in National Sports Marketing Bureau's publication on Ron Wolf, Vice President of the Tampa expansion franchise of the National Football League. While in college, Mr. Wolf subscribed to a football magazine and often wrote to the editor to correct errors and make suggestions. The editor was so impressed with Wolf's suggestions and corrections that he offered him a job. He later recommended Wolf to Al Davis, of the Oakland Raiders. He took Wolf on as an assistant and when Davis became Commissioner of the American Football League, Wolf went with him. When Davis returned to the Raiders, Wolf returned as a personnel director and did a brilliant job of drafting. He landed the Tampa job without even applying for it.

Two brothers from New York, Pete and Carl Marasco also took a unique way into the sports profession. Both loved football and as a hobby began gathering statistics on college seniors. They wrote to practically every college with a football program and watched as many college games as they could. With the huge amount of material they collected, they proceeded to rate the college seniors as to their professional potential. They even predicted the order in which players would be selected in the National League draft. They leaked their predictions to a football magazine, and after seven years of accurately forecasting the draft, they became recognized as experts and left their jobs to take positions in sports administration. Pete Marasco is now a scout for the New York Jets, and Carl Marasco is the personnel director for the Chicago Bears.

These men really entered sports administration via left field but they prove that positions are there for people with imagination, initiative, and determination.

Many front office men at the major league level received their training in the minor leagues. They didn't care who they worked for or how much they made. They just wanted a chance to prove themselves and learn the world of sports from the bottom up.

A good example is Pat Williams, former General Manager of the Philadelphia 76'ers. After playing minor baseball, Mr. Williams went to work for the Spartanburg Phillies, a minor league team in South Carolina. At Spartanburg, he created a promotion for every one of the Phillies 63 home games. The year before Mr. Williams arrived, Spartanburg drew only 46,000 for the entire season. By the time he was ready to move on, attendance soared to a record 173,000 in a county with a population of only 145,000. Pat Williams went on to become Business Manager of the Philadelphia 76'ers and General Manager of the Chicago Bulls, before moving on to Atlanta and then back to Philadelphia. Not everyone has the promotional genious of a Pat Williams, but the major point is that he made his reputation in the minor leagues.

As you read the daily sports pages in your local newspaper or circulated magazine, be aware of recent administration changes or the formation of expansion franchises and developing leagues. Both newly established teams and conferences will have smaller budgets, and depending on the nature of the kind of sport, experienced people will either be hard to come by in this area or those who have expertise will not be willing to accept a lower pay scale. In addition, be alert for athletic departments that are expanding and creating first time positions. Universities are always looking to diversify high salary positions with entry level professional positions in such areas as of public relations and marketing. Splitting job roles this way does not jeopardize the organization, but adds a degree of specialization to augment limited salary budgets.

These are the ideal situations you are looking for since you are not competing in areas of the established franchises where there are many experienced people. The key to your future is getting your "foot in the door."

Another excellent approach to gain valuable experience and possibly get that "foot in the door," is to pursue an internship. Internships are not only granted through educational institutions, but also can be attained by soliciting organizations individually. An internship may include a stipend for your services or can also be contracted through your institution's department advisor for possible course credit. Many executives today were offered positions on account of their exceptional performance that they displayed during their intern period. If you wish to solicit an Internship on your own, consult the directory of this publication for the names and addresses of the organizations you wish to contact. Always try to pursue an area or particular team you would like to work for. You never know what could transpire during that trial period. Never just send a letter, but make an appointment in person with the director or department head. If the franchise or organization is not sold on the idea the first try, be persistent and restate your proposal at another occasion which would appear to be an opportune time during the sports season. Your aggressiveness and tenacity alone could sell your position if the club is that impressed.

Never rule out the obvious such as your local high school or recreation department when developing your plan of action for acquiring experience. If coaching is your forte, then check out the possibility of student coaching for college credit or taking over an athletic program in a private school system. Private schools are not as stringent on awarding coaching positions to only faculty staff members and the opportunity for advancement is much quicker at the high school level. For those of you with college playing experience, numerous graduate assistant-ships are allowed for each intercollegiate team. Unfortunately no salary is involved, but the training and contacts made in the collegiate ranks will prove to be invaluable. Even though these initial years will be of volunteer nature, it's much easier to begin in the collegiate system than trying to mive in from the high school ranks.

If you are still in high school or college, there are numerous opportunities right before your eyes. With the many budget cuts and positions being abolished in our country's learning in-stitutions, many athletic directors would welcome your services in one way or another and possibly provide you with some form of compensation.

Sports editors, statisticians, and publications specialists can always be utilized by sports in-formation directors and departments. Trainers and managers are continually in short supply in both the high school and collegiate circle. Many universities are now offering scholarships for students who work in these areas which very much resemble the aid granted to student athletes.

Numerous part-time and full-time positions are available without prior experience at major auditoriums and arenas as well as country clubs and recreation centers. Not only are you be-ing paid for a job you enjoy doing, but you will be able to rub shoulders and possibly meet influential people with the various events and professional performers that are scheduled. Most of these positions can be accomplished without even giving up your regular income or while you are still completing your education. Don't rule out volunteering your services during na-tional golf or tennis tournaments or even spending your free time around the local race track. By just being helpful and asking questions to the right people, eventually you will be noticed by someone for consideration if you are sincerely honest about pursuing the field of your choice.

A gutsy yet determined approach is to attend national conferences and league meetings. Vince Naus, 1980 graduate of Biscayne College in Miami, Florida (now St. Thomas Univers-ity), attended the 1979 Major Lague Baseball's winter meetings in Toronto, Canada, to learn more about the sport and hopefully develop contacts for future employment. Though the adven-ture was costly, his efforts were not in vain. By mixing with the many franchise repesentatives and presenting his objectives, he landed an intern position with the Amarillo Gold Sox of the Texas Baseball League. Soon after his appointment he was named General Manager of the club for the remainder of the summer season. His accomplishments were so profound that the club's owner made a recommendation to the Baseball Commissioner, Bowie Kuehn, in-dicating that Vince was an aspiring administrator with definite potential. Shortly before gradua-tion at the age of 23, Vince Naus was offered an administrative position in which he reported directly to the Commissioner. He was the youngest individual to ever hold such a position!

Success stories like these are rare. But with determination, you can succeed. For Vince suc-ceeding came at a great sacrifice in time, money and effort. But he persevered in spite of the odds and ultimately reached his goal.

Whenever you come upon a contact or lead, follow it up completely until you are sure it's a dead end. Many letters and long distance telephone calls will only lead to more of the same, but follow them up completely even if you think you are on a wild goose chase. As long as there is another lead or contact to be made — do so.

Unfortunately, openings in sports related positions are probably the least publicized of any occupation. However, one of the most common means of finding job leads in any career is through the process of "networking." The use of networking involves five key steps:

1. *Informational Interview Follow-Ups* — Contact the persons you have interviewed earlier for information and tell that you are now seeking employment in their field. Ask if they know

of any openings or have suggestions of people to contact. Send them a resume, but more importantly, keep in contact with them throughout your job search.

2. *Level Two Informational Interview* — Contact people in the field you have chosen and let them know you are making a career change and would like to talk with them. Some possible topics for the interview are (a) discuss an issue or new development in the field, (b) gain information about their organization, acknowledging that there may not be openings at this time or, (c) ask where someone with your experience would fit into their organization. Ask if they know of any openings or have suggestions of people to contact. Keep in contact with them throughout your job search.

3. *Assertive Interview* — Identify an organization with a need which you can fill. Carefully research the organization and the problems they face. Prepare a proposal of how you can solve a problem or fill a need. Contact the person with the power to hire and present your proposal and qualifications.

4. *Your Personal Network* — Tell everyone you know — friends, relatives, neighbors, insurance agents, hairdressers, clergy, teachers, bankers, creditors, former employers and co-workers, bus riders, school alumni — that you are looking for work. Ask for leads to openings or persons working in the field. Keep them posted on the progress of your search.

5. *Professional Business or Trade Associations* — Attend meetings, volunteer for committees, read their newsletter. Make initial contacts with persons working in the field and follow up with Level Two informational interviews. Never underestimate the value of chamber of commerces and civic organizations as well as calling upon league associations directly. Many times you just may be at the right place at the right time.

As you set out to market your skills, keep in mind that thousands of aspiring enthusiasts like you are also developing dreams. That's why you need to be creative and unique in your career marketing.

Bruce Jenner said it so well when a reporter asked him how it felt to be the "best in the world" after his decathalon victory. His response was "the best in the world is sometwhere out there and doesn't even know it. He's probably sitting behind an office desk right now. The difference is either he doesn't know it or didn't care enough to do anything abut his talent. I'm really not the best in the world, I simply wanted it more than anyone else in the world."

CHAPTER 16

APPLICATION TECHNIQUES

In most situations, you never really "apply" for an athletic related position, because sports organizations, especially professional franchises, literally never publicize an opening. Since openings are so scarce, those who arrive at the right time, whose personalities mix and appear the best qualified, are the ones who are offered positions.

Timing is the key factor in nailing down a job in sports. Many years may pass before key individuals retire or move on to another team. If you, your letter of application, or your resume happen to be sitting on the General Manager's desk at that time, you may get the break you've been waiting for. That's why it is so important to continually follow up on our best leads. Even if you make an infrequent call to an organization for only a few minutes, the object is to keep your name in the back of your contact's mind.

Always read sports sections carefully. Sometimes there will be a hint that an administrator is accepting another position or is ready to retire. Another hint on timing is that most jobs are filled before the season begins as most changes are made at the end of the schedule. Therefore, the best time to contact any team or league office would be just before the conclusion of the season. Also, all intercollegiate athletic openings are circulated to all institutions throughout the country and many can be found posted in athletic business offices. The NCAA weekly newsletter and Education Week are two publications that contain articles concerning current issues in sports and list job openings from around the country in numerous sports-related fields. Though many of these positions have someone already chosen as a replacement, it never hurts to pursue them. However, be weary of new opportunity listings that have deadline application dates close to the posting of the position. These vacancies more than likely are already filled and are advertised merely to meet mandated hiring policies. Still, remember, "nothing ventured, nothing gained."

By now you have the picture that anyone with a developed contacts has the best chance of landing a position since only 18% of all professional managerial, and executive jobs are advertised or listed with agencies, search firms, or newspapers. It makes sense — the more good contacts you make . . . the better opportunities you will have to explore. Never underestimate developing contacts through part-time occupations, social/civic activities, local influentials, past athletic acquaintances, or even during major sporting events.

Once you have decided where to apply for a sports-related position, you need to develop a cover letter and prepare a resume for the job you are pursuing.

The cover letter is very important and should accompany all resumes. Its main purpose is to introduce you to your potential employer and to get him to read your resume. It is important that you adhere to the following guidelines:

1. It must be neat, grammatically correct and it should be typed. Your objective is to make

your first impression a good one. Never use mimeographed form letters, and if at all possible, select paper and letterhead for a professional touch.

2. Address the letter to a specific person. A letter is more likely to be taken seriously when it is addressed to an individual. This is why we have included in our directory (if possible) the name of either the general manager or the owner of the various teams. If you are applying to an organization not listed in the directory, call its office and ask the secretary for the name of the man or woman in charge of personnel.

3. The first paragraph of your letter is very important. In these few words you must make the reader want to continue reading. Try to get the reader's attention but don't use a cute expression or cliche. Never abbreviate any words and type every word in its entirety. Since you are applying for a serious position, a light approach will not be appreciated.

4. Highlight your educational or business background.

5. Let the organization know that you are willing to work and all you want is chance. Be sincere. Enthusiasm for the industry and the career field is vital.

6. Always ask for a personal interview. If it is a local organization, you may even suggest that you will telephone them for an interview.

7. Above all, you must impress the reader that you have something to offer the organization. This is what all organizations are looking for — someone above the grade to make a positive contribution.

8. Keep your letter brief and to the point. You are just summarizing your career while your resume will fill in the details.

Included are some sample letters from a typical student and a businessman with a background of considerable experience. When reviewing the letters, take a close look at the opening and closing paragraphs as well as the words that have been used as a means of persuasion. While you shouldn't just copy these samples, you should be able to directly borrow words phrases, sentences, and paragraphs and creatively adapt their use to your own background.

Though you will usually accompany your letter with a resume, the combination of the two will rarely produce as many interviews as a well-written letter. In a letter you can tailor your presentation, discuss what you can do, or arouse curiousity. Besides, resumes, if not designed very impressionable, make it easier for readers to discover a reason for disqualifying you.

SAMPLE LETTER FROM STUDENT CONTACTING EMPLOYERS

1983 Opportunity Street
Philadelphia, PA 19104
June 30, 1982

Mr. George Washington, President
Philadelphia Freedom
1 Liberty Square
Philadelphia, PA 19104

Dear Mr. Washington:

Philadelphia Freedom's reputation as a first class organization has inspired me to contact you regarding possible employment opportunities. I feel I have the potential, the enthusiasm and the training to step in and immediately make a positive contribution to your organization.

I am a recent graduate of Biscayne College where I have taken specialized courses in the area of sports administration. I have also worked the past two years on a part-time basis, as an assistant to the public relations director at Sporting Goods International. My earnings from that position enabled me not only to finance my education, but also to gain valuable experience in communications and in dealing with the sports public.

In my part-time capacity, I have been exposed to a variety of public relations problems, and have learned how to deal creatively with them. In the absence of a senior executive, I was given complete responsibility for company relations with local recreational groups.

The field of sports has always fascinated me and I want very much to make it my lifetime occupation. I am willing to take any available position or project in order to break into your organization.

Enclosed is a copy of my resume. I look forward to meeting you personally at your convenience.

Thank you for your consideration.

Sincerely,

Paul Revere

Enclosure

SAMPLE LETTER FROM EXPERIENCED APPLICANT FOR CONTACTING EMPLOYERS

Dear_____

The enclosed resume highlighting my advertising background may be of interest to you should an opening occur in your public relations or promotion department.

As a professional with five years successful experience, I thought that my experience in this field might be of interest to you.

Some of my recent accomplishments include:

-Selection to the National Promotions Advisory Board.

-Management of the third largest promotional campaign in the _____ inustry.

-Compilation of an industry-wide media guide that will soon be published for the public.

I am 36 years old, married and have three children. I have a BS (1978) from the University of Minnesota and an MA (1981) from Boston University in advertising. Relocation and travel requirements present no problem.

I have always been interested in the field of sports and feel I could adapt my knowledge of advertising to help promote your franchise.

I am confident that you will find a personal meeting at your convenience both interesting and mutually beneficial. I look forward to seeing if I can present some exciting ideas with the challenges you face ahead.

Sincerely,

Paul Revere

Enclosure

RESUME

Your resume should be a summary of your education and work experience. I can't read that. Your resume is the tool by which you may attain the personal interview which is so vital to your chances of success. The purpose of the resume is to get you that interview. It will also serve as the main topic of conversation during your interview.

1. OBJECTIVE

Your career objective is the first thing that appears on a resume. It should define your employment goals clearly and concisely. Just to say that you want a position in Sports Administration is not enough. You must define the area of Sports Administration in which you would most likely be an asset and justify your choice. Be concise but do not limit your availability.

2. SUMMARY OF QUALIFICATIONS

This section of your resume should include a few of the outstanding highlights of your career. It is a tool for attracting attention. Through these highlights you will be showing how you can make a contribution.

3. EDUCATION

The detail required in the educational section of your resume will depend on what stage of your business career you are in. If you are an upcoming or recent graduate, then your education background should dominate. Give as much information as possible. List your major and minor subjects and if you had a good grade average include this information also. Add all extra-curricular activities to show you are a well-rounded individual. For those who have a long work history, the education section of the resume need not be as complete. If you have completed college, list dates, name of college, location, and degree earned. Always list the top level of schooling first. If you attended graduate school list that first. If you entered the business world directly from high school, list dates, name of school and type of diploma you received. Even if your education is limited, do not leave it out. If you have taken home study courses or night school courses, include them. They will show a willingness on your part to work and learn.

4. EMPLOYMENT

When listing your employment record, start with your most current jobs and work backgrounds. Include starting and leaving dates, name of company, your position, and a brief summary of your duties. For the new graduate, list all part-time and summer work applicable to your field of interest. It is important to show that you have had some business experience. For the experienced worker, this is the heart of your resume and you should point out your career achievements. Salaries need not be stated in your resume. In fact if you do, you will often limit your bargaining power. Salary will be discussed at the interview so save it until that time.

5. PERSONAL INFORMATION

It is important to give your potential employer a certain amount of personal data since you are trying to present a complete picture of yourself. Since you have probably never met the hiring party and your resume only lists some of your achievements, this personal section tells him more about you as an individual. It should include your date and place of birth, height and weight, your marital status, number of children (if any), type of residence, hobbies, clubs or social affiliations, and your service record. If your military service was extensive it may appear in the employment section of your resume.

These are the basic ingredients of a good resume. Don't leave out any important information but be sure it is stated in a clear, concise, believable manner. Keep in mind, you are communicating with a knowledgeable, busy executive who will not wade through pages of detail. Always try to be factual. If the director of employment is interested in you, chances are that someone will check the accuracy of the information you submit.

SAMPLE RESUME

Paul A. Revere
1983 Opportunity Street
Philadelphia, PA 19104
Phone: (404) 377-0247 (B) 624-7301

EMPLOYMENT OBJECTIVE

Position in sports administration leading to franchise administration in public relations or promotions.

SUMMARY OF QUALIFICATIONS

Educational background concentrated in business administration with emphasis in personnel psychology and relations. Sports administration minor specializing in public relations, sports psychology, and wellness fitness programs.

Familiarity gained through promotional and fund raising procedures gained with experience as program coordinator with a major university.

My strongest personal assets are self-discipline, strong communication skills, aggressiveness, and a personable disposition. My main attributes are the ability to organize, innovate, and deal with the public while at the same time being able to be very influential.

EDUCATION

1980 graduate of Freedom College, Philadelphia, Pennsylvania.

Received a Bachelor of Science in Personnel Administration and a minor in Sports Administration. Electives have been predominately in industrial relations with emphasis in psychology/sociology departments. Scholastic record: 3.0 (out of 4.0) in Major Field; 3.7 in Minor Field.

1978 graduate of Biscayne College, Miami, Florida.

Considered one of the best sports administration programs in the country. Completed 24 credits towards my minor in sports administration at Biscayne College, Miami, Fla. Earned recognition to be on the Dean's list.

1975 graduate of Valley Forge High School, Boston, Massachusetts:

Graduated 25th out of 250 in a college prepatory, military school. Member of the concert and marching bands as well as receiving the rank of officer in the R.O.T.C. junior program.

INTERVIEW

If your introductory letter and resume do their job, you may be called for apersonal interview. This first personal contact will be extremely important in promoting chances for employment.

Before the interview form a strategy that will allow you a partial lead in the meeting. Begin by making sure that you are on time. Sports professionals are busy people and if you are late, it will cut into your allotted time or force you to be cancelled out all together.

In either event, it will probably be a strike against you if you are late. Dress conservatively. While you often see professional athletes wearing the most outrageous clothes, owners and the administrators are usually conservative. Remember, conservative attire will not offend anyone while a gaudy outfit may rub someone the wrong way. Always wear a darker colored suit with a tie. Keep your hair medium length — and while beards and mustaches are now accepted — the opinion of this publication is to be clean shaven. Try to maintain an athletic, healthy physical image. Though you can't be discriminated for this, it sure can help.

As for the interview itself, try to be at ease. Everyone will be a little nervous at first but you must realize that the General Manager, or whoever is doing the interview, is human too and must be interested in you or else wouldn't be seeing you. Questions will be based on your letter and resume, so it's a good idea for you to study these documents before the interview so the details are fresh in your mind. Try to be as educated as possible about the interviewing organization especially in regards to its current issues and the position you are applying for. Each interview and interviewer is different, but these things should help you in just about any situation:

Before the Interview

1. Research and attempt to find out as much as possible about the position that is available. If possible, request that a job description be sent to you. Talk to your contacts in the organization for additional information.

2. Research the organization or institution. Find out as much as possible about the organization's history and philosophy. Talk with your contacts who work with the company or who are familiar with it.

3. Research yourself. Based on what you know about the opening and the company, make a list of strengths and skills needed for the job. Now consider your experiences, skills and strengths. Identify specific examples of activities or work experiences where you used or gained the skills or knowledge you listed as necessary for the position. Write down 3-4 major points that you want the employer to know about you and your experience.

4. Anticipate the possible questions that you may be asked during the interview and formulate your answers. Practice answering the questions.

5. Prepare questions to ask of the employer. Consider what you want to know about the position and the company. Write the questions down and bring them with you to the interview.

6. Bring with you to the interview:
   (1) Extra copy of your resume
   (2) Typed list of your references
   (3) Portfolio of examples of your work
   (4) Your questions for the employer

7. Consider what you will wear. Choose comfortable, business-like clothes appropriate for the position.

During the Interview:

1. Be polite, present a sincere nature, wear a quick smile, and display an interesting and enthusiastic personality. Keep in mind that the purpose of the interview is an exchange of information, not an inquisition.

2. Arrive 5-10 minutes early.

3. Have a firm grip when shaking hands and always maintain direct eye contact.

4. Be frank and answer all questions asked. If you do not know the answer to a particular question, say so; don't try to fake it.

5. Be alert and eager. Never appear bored or disinterested. Try to keep the conversation concentrated on your positive achievements and how you can help the organization.

6. Don't exaggerate your achievements. It's easy to check any extraordinary claims you make.

7. Be a good listener and if time permits, ask intelligent questions about the organization.

8. If your strategy about leading the interview does not work, don't fight it. Let the interviewer lead. You must be a good listener as well as a talker. Don't fall into the trap of formulating answers or rebuttals in your mind while the interviewer is talking.

9. Don't rush your answers. After a question is posed, it is not necessary to give an instant answer. Take a few seconds to organize your thoughts and then give a direct answer.

10. Be consistent and truthful. Don't agree with an interviewer just because he says something. No organization likes just "yes" men, so you don't have to agree with everything. On the other hand, don't go out of your way to disagree with everything just to show your independence.

11. Don't dwell on your past experience. Find out what the new position requires and point out how you can apply your know-how to it.

12. Don't try to "snow" your interviewer with your sport knowledge or name dropping. He/she probably knows more than you and is looking for a worker, not a fan.

13. Never beg for a position. Organizations are looking for individuals who are in demand and have something unique to offer.

14. Speak well of your present employer. If you speak poorly about him, then your potential employer may feel you will do the same to them.

15. Always follow up with a thank you letter to show your appreciation and concern with the organization. It could be the touch to make the difference.

16. Remember that there are many people looking for jobs in sports and you must show the interviewer that you are more eager, sincere, and serious than the others, and that you are willing to start anywhere just for the chance to make a positive contribution to the organization.

If You Get the Job:
1. Notify your contacts and references that you have taken a new job and thank them for their assistance.

If You Don't Get the Job:
1. Contact the person who interviewed you and ask her/him to give you feedback about your experience and interviewing skills that may help to improve your job search.

2. If you are still interested in the organization, send a letter stating your interest and maintain contact with them to learn of future openings.

CHAPTER 17

SWITCHING CAREERS TO A SPORTS-RELATED OCCUPATION

To this point, the emphasis of this publication has been on aspiring students seeking sports-related careers. But what are the possibilities for the individual with years of experience in a non-athletic career? Can someone with no specific sports training make a new start in the world of sports?

Actually, depending upon the field you choose, your other professional experience can be viewed as an advantage. Earlier it was mentioned that it is important to begin developing a career during a youthful age. This has been proven to be the most effective route since usually a minimum of responsibilities and liabilities exist in one's early 20s which should allow for more extensive soul searching and risk taking. Unfortunately, even though a recent graduate may discover his/her true career endeavor, the greatest drawback to youth, its lack of experience and unproven potential may raise the eyebrows of the future employer. Though individuals in their mid-life or later years may not be as easily retrained or as willing to pay the journeyman dues like their younger counterparts, what they do possess is established know-how and "street sense" which can't be taught in books — it must be lived.

In the chapter "Where To Go For Training," it is stated that a curriculum in sports administration will amount to nothing more than a business administration degree performed in a sports environment. This can be exemplified by examining a professional franchise which is in search of a public relations director. The recruiting process will not involve a list of young interns fresh out of school, but usually will include administrators with 20 years or more experience from the corporate world. This is not to say that an intern or graduate may not be approached to be an assistant or possibly a protege, only that when push comes to shove, experience conquers all.

Joe Robbi, owner of the Miami Dolphins, intentionally moved his club offices to a distant location from the team's practice facility to alleviate the distractions of the environment. For those of you who feel sports related careers are all entertainment and in the spot light, please picture yourself employed in a similar type position in a corporate setting as a gauge to your job expectations. Game day is showtime for the performers, not the support staff.

Characteristically, sports specific occupations require a more specialized knowledge and many times a certain type of personality which make these positions both unique and demanding. This is why since such fields as sports medicine and sports psychology have been precise sciences that practicing physicians and clinical psychologists without higher training in these specialized areas would be providing an injustice to their patients and clients who would request such services. Partaking in symposiums, clinics, and workshops, in addition to attending seminars and taking coursework at institutions that offer specialized curriculums, will provide meaningful insight and application techniques into the practices of these already successful professionals.

For those who are hesitant about making a complete switch into a sports career, utilizing the informational interview first and then acquiring experience either on a part-time or volunteer nature, will enable the individual to make a slow career transition while still maintaining the security of an income for "testing the waters" in the sports market. Whenever an individual has made the choice to switch careers, sports related or otherwise, it is imperative to have a plan of action for a smooth turnover. Briefly stated, never quit an established job just on a whim much less dive into a life style change without having a course of action outlined which will suffice your personal, family, and career goals.

Accountants, business managers, marketing specialists, or for that matter any one of several other sports related occupations, perform basically the same functions as similar type positions in education, government, or private business. However, the one distinct difference is that the world of sports careers may be viewed as more glamorous and enjoyable. The flip side to this mystique can be attributed to the drawbacks of the supply and demand principles. Since so many members of the work force are willing to take a sports position no matter what the costs, usually the salary and benefits will be less than those of comparable positions elsewhere. The possible exceptions to this rule are the highly technical fields such as physical therapy, exercise physiology, or sports nutrition, which may demand higher salary figures due to their relative uniqueness and scarcity.

When applying for a sports-type position for the first time, review the section in this book on resume writing for the experienced businessman. In the cover letter market your already existing skills and emphasize your enthusiasm and commitment to athletics by your involvement with coursework and seminars applicable to furthering yourself in the field you are applying. When interviewing, make it a point in your strategy to express how your sports knowledge of current issues coupled with your past experience will be an additional asset and provide a new dimension into the organization. Throughout the cover letter and functional resume for a specific position, emplore sports terminology and "buzz words" which give the application an athletic flavor. This may be accomplished by using terms such as sports information instead of statistics, or sports studies rather than physical education. This technique may provide the touch that attracts the interviewer.

A solid and successful non-sports related background is of much greater value and attraction to an employer than a resume which is very sports oriented but lacks a successful work record. Therefore being around athletics all your life isn't as important as associating oneself with accomplished and established work principles. When approaching a vacancy the question to be asked is not "what can the employer do for me," but "what can I offer to the employer?"

CHAPTER 18

WOMEN IN SPORTS

Ever since the enactment of Title IX in 1972, the female athlete has increasingly established her place in the world of sports. With this on surge of interest & enthusiasm, an inexhaustible number of career opportunities have been created in the marketplace to meet this new demand. Much like the sudden participation boom with amateur soccer that arose in the late '70s, likewise women's sports initially faced a comparable crisis of not having enough qualified female personnel to coach, officiate, or even administer their programs. Even though many of these positions could have easily been absorbed by experienced male counterparts (and many conceivably were), when given the opportunity, women sports program directors have indicated a definite preference to hire female staff members almost to the point of appearing to be reverse-discriminatory.

With the increased emphasis of women's sports in the 80s, additional opportunities in sports related careers other than the more traditional roles of coaching, physical education instruction, and administration have developed. The current demand for the more prestigious roles such as journalists, TV color commentators, sports medicine practitioners, and athletic counselors now rivals that for the male sports professional. The only area in which women have not achieved career stability and financial success is that of performing in the capacity as a professional athlete. In as much as the need for trained female professionals will continue to rise in nearly all facets of sports careers, the likelihood of women athletes sustaining professional status on a full-time basis remains poor.

Salary considerations for womens sports positions have steadily become more competitive in recent years but still are not on par with comparable male titles. As more competitively trained women gradually enter the sports marketplace, the need for male expertise will conversely dwindle. This substitution process will allow women to assume the salaries once paid to their male constituents which will result in a higher compensation structure.

Women sports enthusiasts should approach the sports job market much in the same fashion that males would. One word of caution though as there still exists sports organizations as well as certain geographic locations around the United States that still believe that any involvement in the key sports positions should be relegated to the white male.

Women like many other minorities must understand, but not accept, that the professional sports hierarchy is represented by a much more traditional structure that is conservative in its mode of thinking. In recent times the controlling forces of professional sport have been under constant scrutiny to reconsider their hiring and "fraternity like" policies in both coaching & administration positions.

To further illustrate professional sports' lack of progressive thinking, the amateur and Olympic levels of competition are usually years ahead of the professional ranks in terms of utilizing state-of-the-art technological advancements and coaching techniques. The professional arena's somewhat conservative approach to management & performance enhancement can be reflected by the fact that it will usually be the last tier of sports participation to implement innovative changes.

Considering that securing employment in the sports arena presents some unique obstacles for the female job seeker, the following tips shoved provide assistance in pursuing a career endeavor:

- Network with as many students & professionals that you know who are employed in sports at both the profit & non-profit levels. Don't on the other hand shy away from groups or organizations which are male dominated since it may be your continued diligence that may provide the impetus to break the established pattern.

- Become involved & learn more about female sports organizations. When contemplating an entry level position, these groups will usually provide your first line of employment opportunity.

- Become knowledgeable in all aspects of sports issues and current trends in both women and men's activities. Never limit your expertise to one topic or sport.

- Secure an internship even if it does not provide monetary compensation. Considering that most female events and non-profit groups operate on a limited budget, if you happen to have a knack for fund-raising, no matter what field of interest you choose to pursue this talent will be an invaluable asset.

- Attend different types of female sports activities & introduce yourself to the key people. Be assertive in meeting the organizers and the performing athletes. Since it is this type of contact which may be able to supply a personal recommendation in the future.

- Subscribe to female oriented sports periodicals to increase your awareness of the market's opportunities.

Organizations that will provide you with insights into the women's sports scene include:

National Association for Girls & Women in Sport

This professional group serves as an informational source for events, issues, and developments for women in sports. The membership is composed of both young and old alike in numerous areas including coaching, physical education, officiating, athletic training, and administration.

For more information, contact:

National Association for Girls & Women in Sport
1900 Association Drive
Reston, VA 22091

(703) 476-3450

Women's Sports Foundation

The Women's Sports Foundation is America's foremost organization for the promotion and future development of women in sport. To accomplish its goal of providing females of all ages the benefits of a physically active lifestyle, the WSF utilizes the following programs.

- *Education* Awareness and knowledge increased through its Speaker Bureau, Women's Sports Hall of Fame, Public Service Announcements, and High School All Star Awards.

- *Opportunity* Girls and women are given an opportunity to discover their potential through the availability of The Travel and Training Fund, The Sport Camp Scholarship Program, and The WSF Internship Program.

• *Advocacy* The WSF provides information through referral services, quarterly newsletters, conferences, and serves as a support group to further legislation that affects women in sport. For more information, contact:

Womens Sports Foundation
342 Madison Ave.
S-728
New York, NY 10017

1-(800) 227-3988
(212) 972-9170

Women's Sports & Fitness Magazine

With the rise of women's participation in athletics and the appearance of women on male teams, this has become an attractive publication. The magazine covers every aspect of sports participation and performance from personal features to advancements in sports psychology and sports medicine. Highly informative, it is a must for both the young and experienced female enthusiast.

Subscription information, contact:

Women's Sport Publications Inc.
310 Town & Country Village
Palo Alto, CA 94301

(415) 321-5102

CHAPTER 19

CONCLUSION AND TIPS

Realistically your success in the sports profession depends on your diligence. Don't let letters of rejection get you down — you will receive many of them. If a team tells you that there are no openings at the present time, but will talk to you in person if you like, by all means do it. Follow up all leads and if someone in sports does see you, be sure and write a letter of thanks for his or her time. Your chances really depend on yourself.

Keep in mind: Are you willing to write to all these organizations? Are you willing to work anywhere, doing anything? Are you willing to start out at a modest salary? And are you willing to keep trying when the odds are against you and the rejections are piling up?

Career Steps: Summing It All Up

- Evalueate yourself. You know you love sports, but are you ready to devote yourself to them in connection with a career? Make sure you are not transforming a fun, energizing part of your life into a daily grind.

- Set your goals. You must decide what you want to be. Then let this aspiration guide you in a general direction following through, with the information you learned here. Write to the professional organizations listed for the fields that interest you, talk to people who are already in the field, head for the library and read applicable journals and other publications. Think about what you want in terms of salary, responsibilities, location, and advancement opportunities, and think about what talents you have to offer and what interests you want to pursue. Career planning is a process — you may not know exactly what you want right away, but the better defined your goal, the easier the rest of the process becomes.

- Continually update your personal inventory (taking stock) and stay in touch with your personal, family, and career goals. Revert back to the dream career model and constantly evaluate your needs and priorities. Soul search now before you leap into an adventure that may not be right for you. If in doubt, visit a career counselor. Seeing a counselor now, who you trust, is advantageous and more efficient than seeing him/her later when the consequences are much more expensive in all respects.

- Get the education you need. No matter where you are in your education — high school junior, college freshman or with schooling far behind you — you'll need to meet an employer's bottom-line educational requirements. If you're still in high school, now's the time to start planning. If you've already graduated from college, you may have to backtrack or supplement your education with additional schooling. As this guide makes clear, some careers have

137

firm educational prerequisites; for others, there are recommended courses of study. Your career research and the advice of guidance counselors can help you construct a program to fit your needs. Keep your career goal in mind when you choose your electives and extra-curricular activities.

- Get experience. Internships, work-study, part-time and summer jobs are all good sources of experience that can help you prepare for a career. Almost any real-world job experience will gain you points by showing that you can tackle projects, take on responsibility, and deal with people and deadlines. But like your education, the more directed this type of experience is and the more connected it is to your goals, the more impressive it will be on a job application or resume. You can also use work experiences as a laboratory to test your career goals and add information to your job research files.

    Remember that sports experience helps. If your competitive specialty jives with your career goals, so much the better. The value of "on hands" experience can never be underestimated whether it be sports related or not. But even the general lessons you learn in sports — teamwork, how to win and lose, the value of competition — will be among your best selling points no matter what career or line of work you choose.

- Get into the job market. Once your diploma is in hand and you've buttressed it with experience, you're ready to attack the job market. Again, the first step is research. Look for entry level positions that can be paths to your career goal. Update the research you did before (and this time let the groups and individuals know that you are looking for work) and check the standard job listings — newspapers, magazines, placement services. Don't forget word of mouth.

    Once you decide what jobs you want to aim for, prepare a resume — a listing of your educational and work experience designed to emphasize your best attributes. Keep it short, simple, appealing, and directed as specifically as possible toward the job or jobs you want.

- Be aggressive. There is a long-standing job-hunting dictum: follow every lead no matter what direction it takes you and stop only if you are convinced it has reached a dead end. Send your resume to all the possible job sources your research unearthed — whether or not you know a job is available. Getting a job is sometimes just a matter of being in the right place at the right time, and you should do everything you can to make sure you're the "lucky" one.

    Try to get in to talk to people, briefly, even if there is no specific job available. At the least, it's another form of research. At the most, the in-person impression you make now may pay off when an opening does occur later. Present yourself to a prospective employer positively and with a cooperative, I'm willing to work hard attitude. Don't be afraid to ask questions; stress your strongest qualifications and let the interviewer know why you think you'd be good in the job.

The field of professional athletics is fiercely competitive, and the number of good jobs limited. Be prepared for disappointments and be prepared to keep trying. Peggy Flemming, who has been able to juggle more than one sports career, offers this advice: "Keep a positive attitude. Don't allow yourself to be discouraged over small failures. Nothing significant has ever been achieved easily."

And by the way, good luck.

CHAPTER 20

MAGAZINES & NEWSPAPERS

The following list of nationally sold publications which will provide indepth knowledge of current trends, issues, and happenings of the magazine's topic matter. Not only will you acquire a better understanding of the publication's focus, but the possibility also exists that you may discover potential contacts and leads to future employment through the reading of each. Most publishers will usually send you one complimentary inspection copy if you write the editor directly especially if it is not a common newsstand item.

For the first time, a single publication will report on the people, transactions, competitive dynamics and special characteristics that make up this unique industry.

Sports Inc., The Sports Business Weekly has perspectives for all those who earn their livelihood in the business of sports, whether in sports marketing, manufacturing, promotion, corporate sponsorship, stadium management, college and high school sports, advertising, professional ownership, management and agentry, medicine, law and the world of the media.

Before listing each publication alphabetically, the editor would like to endorse what he feels will be the premier magazine of its kind for the serious "student of sport." To subscribe to this weekly publication, write:

> Sports Inc., The Sports Business Weekly
> P.O. Box 1564
> Neptune, NJ 07754-9918

Athletic Journal 1719 Howard Street
Evanston, IL 60202
(312) 328-8545

Established in 1921 this journal is written monthly by coaches for coaches. Highly technical in its format, it does offer a wide variety of sports portrayed.

Baseball Digest 1020 Church Street
Evanston, IL 60201

Like its sister magazines (*Hockey, Football, Basketball,* and *Soccer*), Century Publishing's compact "bible" has everything the sports enthusiast could ask for in a reading format.

The Basketball Clinic *Parker Publishing Company*
West Nyack, NY 10994

A highly technical and expensive periodical that features articles by successful coaches. This publication should be ordered by libraries in communities where the reading public is totally committed to baskeball. This company publishes similar journals for other sports.

Basketball News   114 Madison Avenue
                                     Coral Gables, FL 33134

A weekly newspaper that publishes extensive information on all aspects of the sport. It appeals more to the player than to the spectator.

Basketball Weekly   19830 Mack Avenue
                                     Grosse Pointe, MI 48236

A weekly newspaper published seasonally that contains an enormous amount of information on the sport. In addition to statistical information, each issue contains in-depth articles on teams, coaches, and players at the secondary, college, and professional level.

Bicycling   119 Paul Drive
                                     San Rafael, CA 94903
                                     (215) 967-5171

With the expansion of interest in cycling, librarians might wish to consider this purchase. It contains articles on everything from saddle soreness to desert biking with the recreational & serious rider in mind.

Black Sports   31 East 28th Street
                                     New York, NY 10016

A sports journal that concentrates on black athletes, mainly professional but also features college and high school players. In addition to addressing issues and concerns of black athletes, it offers technical articles, book reviews, and many fine illustrated pictures.

Boating   P.O. Box 2773
                                     Boulder, CO 80302

A lavishly illustrated, well-written, and edited magazine that deals with all aspects of maritime life. In addition to containing the "how to" articles, it also carries adventure, historical, and topical items.

Bowling Digest   P.O. Box 3306
                                     Harlan, IA 51593-2063

This bi-monthly publication is the only magazine of its kind devoted to the bowling enthusiast. Information on league registrations, technique tips, and tournament schedules are featured.

Coach & Athlete   200 S. Hull Street
                                     Montgomery, AL 36104

A very popular publication, especially among high school coaches. Technical articles along with current issues commentary are featured.

Cyclist   P.O. Box 907
                                     Farmingdale, NY 11737-9607
                                     (213) 328-5700

Nine issues each year are published on this magazine which has fulfilled the many long awaited needs of avid cyclists who compete on the local and national levels.

Football News   19830 Mack Avenue
                                     Grosse Pointe, MI 48236

This weekly newspaper circulated during the fall season covers every facet of football at the scholastic level. Each issue contains in-depth articles on coaches, players, and teams with features on philosophies and techniques.

Golf Digest   495 Westport Ave.
                                     Norwalk, CT 06856
                                     (203) 847-5811

For the golfer who likes to read a magazine from cover to cover, this is it. Informative and entertaining, each month of *Gold Digest* will provide a variety of insights into the golf scene.

Golf Illustrated Golf Illustrated
P.O. Box 6057

Published 8 times annually, GI's long tradition continues by covering all facets of golf — the tournament scenes and personalities. Equipment, rules, resorts and fashion as well as techniques in the performance of the game.

Golf Times Mirror Magazine
Box 2786
Boulder, CO 80322

Published monthly, *Golf* is the player's complete information magzine. Whether it be personal features, instructional tips, tour schedules, or reports on the latest equipment, *Golf* presents excellent in-depth reading material.

Hot Rod Magazine Peterson Publishing Co.
5959 Hollywood Blvd.
Los Angeles, CA 90028

Highlighting pictures of customized cars (regular cars that have been remodeled to look more beautiful or adjusted to go faster), this magazine will appeal to any student considering a career in this area.

High School Sports 1230 Avenue of the Americas
New York, NY some of this is not readable

The National Federation of State High School Associations is published bi-monthly (5 times) during the school. *High School Sports* provides excellent reading for both the scholastic coach and student with sports features and profiles on student-athletes from coast to coast.

Inside Sports P.O. Box 3308
Harlan, IA 51593-2065
(312) 491-6440

Personal features with inside information is the trademark of *Inside Sports.* For those wishing to stay abreast with current issues and trends, this monthly magazine has it all.

International Gymnastics Sundby Sports, Inc.
410 Broadway
Santa Monica, CA 90401

Published monthly, this magazine covers the entire international gymnastics scene and is best known for its personal features and its many action packed photos of male and female gymnasts.

Karate Illustrated 1847 W. Empire Avenue
Burbank, CA 91504

This magazine gives proper attention to the martial arts and the people who have made the sport what it is today. It provides excellent reading and graphic photos which would appeal to all sports enthusiasts.

MotoCross Action P.O. Box 9502
Mission Hills, CA 91345-9985

Printed monthly in the heart of Motorcross country, the publication is more of an information guide of who's who, or what's happening for the avid competitor.

Motor Trend Magazine Peterson Publishing Co.
5959 Hollywood Blvd.
Los Angeles, CA 90028

This magazine, which emphasizes safety in the design and manufacture of automobiles, is characterized by pictures and analysis of motor vehicles (gas mileage, handling, braking).

Muscle & Fitness   P.O. Box 4009
                                                      Woodland Hills, CA 91367

Published monthly, *Muscle & Fitness* appeals to the serious body builder or fitness buff who is seeking the latest trends and advancements.

National Coach   3423 E. Silver Springs Blvd., S-9
                                                      Ocala, FL 32670

A newspaper, published by the National High School Athletic Coaches Association that contains techniques and stories related to coaching sports at the high school level. A must for future scholastic coaches!

Runner   P.O. Box 2730
                                                      Boulder, CO 80321

Dedicated to the running advocate, *Runner* is best known to provide insight into trends and advancements before they become commonplace.

Runner's World   Emmaus, PA 18099-0055

One of the pioneers in providing running enthusiasts with first hand information, *Runner's World* has established a fine reputation in its feature articles and in promoting the sport itself.

Running Commentary   Emmaus, PA 18099-0069

Published bi-monthly, this circulation provides the latest running news on events and current happenings.

Running Times   P.O. Box 6509
                                                      Syracuse, NY 13217

Known as "America's Road Running Magazine," this unique publication features topics in fitness, sports medicine, technique, apparel, and even a calendar of events.

Scholastic Coach   Scholastic Coach, Inc.
                                                      50 W. 44th Street
                                                      New York, NY 10036

A fine journal written predominantly for the coach and the mature player, although it should appeal to spectators as well. Contains some technical articles, but the focal point is on submitted editorials.

Skin Diver   Peterson Publishing Co.
                                                      5959 Hollywood Blvd.
                                                      Los Angeles, CA 90028

This magazine features articles on skin diving, places of interest, equipment, and technique. Many have found that their underwater experience was tapped after reading this publication for the first time.

Soccer Digest   P.O. Box 3305
                                                      Harlan, IA 51593-2057

America's only soccer publication is published bi-monthly and covers both the amateur and international scene. *Soccer Digest* is equally enjoyed by both the competitor and spectator.

Sport   McFadden-Bartell Corporation
                                                      205 E. 42nd Street
                                                      New York, NY 10017

Presently edited by the well-known sports journalist, Dick Shaap, this magazine offers many good articles for spectators on the major and minor sports. Feature articles deal with players, coaches, and teams usually in the professional scene.

Sporting News   1212 North Lindbergh
                                         St. Louis, MO 63166

A weekly newspaper that focuses on sports by season. Coverage emphasizes major sports at the professional and collegiate level. Excellent source of statistical information (e.g., baseball batting averages). For the sports trivia minded individual.

Sports Illustrated   541 North Fairbanks Court
                                         Chicago, IL 60611

The largest selling sports magazine in the U.S., *Sports Illustrated* is characterized by crisp writing and excellent pictures. While largely devoted to the spectator sports, it frequently will feature nearly every sport imaginable from around the world.

Sports Women   119 Paul Drive
                                         Rafael, CA 94903

Presenting articles on players, coaches, and techniques, this magazine is especially appropriate for today's female athlete who enjoys informative and entertaining reading in one publication.

Swim Magazine   523 S. 26th Rd.
                                         Arlington, VA 22202
                                         (703) 549-6388

This publication which is published 6 times annually is best known for its attention given towards adult fitness and competitive swimmers. ($12.00 per year)

Swimming World   Swimming World, Inc.
                                         8622 Bellanca
                                         Los Angeles, CA 90045

Magazines like this one and others similar to it (*Boating, Ski, World Tennis, Bicycling, Backpacking Journal, Hockey World, Karate Illustrated,* and *Fishing World*) are useful purchases for libraries where the school or the community has a particular interest in that sport. These magazines contain graphic photography, feature articles, and illustrations beneficial to players, coaches, and teams alike.

Track and Field News   P.O. Box 296
                                         Los Altos, CA 94022
                                         (415) 948-8188

A journal featuring information of interest to athlete and coach. The journal has both technical articles and general information on meets and athletes.

Triathlete   Triathlete Publishers Inc.
                                         1127 Hamilton Street
                                         Allentown, PA 18102
                                         (215) 821-6864

Published on a monthly basis, this magazine is a must for anyone remotely interested in the sport of triathalons. Each issue contains articles focusing on training strategies and techniques divided in the areas of swimming, cycling, and running in addition to articles addressing various areas of interest, controversial issues, new products, and an extensive calendar listing events in the nation and around the world. ($19.95 per year)

Ultra Sport   Raben Ultrasport Partners
                                                        711 Boylston St.
                                                        Boston, MA 02116
                                                        (617) 236-1885

Published monthly "The Magazine of the New Vitality" covers up-to-date advancements in
both fitness and sport. Features and editorials are exceptionally well done and will appeal to
a wide range of audiences.

Volleyball Monthly   Straight Down Inc.
                                                        P.O. Box 3137
                                                        San Luis Obispo, CA 93403
                                                        (805) 541-2294

Winning: Bicycle Racing Illustrated   1127 Hamilton Street
                                                        Allentown, PA 18102

The cyclist's complete informational magazine targeted for the serious or elite racer.

Women Sports & Fitness   Women's Sport Publications Inc.
                                                        310 Town & Country Village
                                                        Palo Alto, CA 94301
                                                        (415) 321-5102

With the rise of women's participation in athletics and the appearance of women on male teams,
this has become an attractive publication. The magazine covers every aspect of sports participation and performance from personal features to advancements in sports psychology and
sports medicine. Highly informative, it is a must for both the young and experienced female
enthusiast.

World Boxing   London Publishing, Inc.
                                                        Box 48
                                                        Rockville Centre, NY 11571

This publication fulfills the need created by the resurgence of boxing. Highly recommended
for the competitor as well as the spectator.

World Tennis   383 Madison Avenue
                                                        New York, NY 10017

For librarians in communities where there is a tennis emphasis, this magazine is a must. It
publishes articles with pictures and diagrams on the leading figures in tennis and technical
essays on how to improve one's game. Content material will appeal to the spectator, instructor,
and player no matter what level of ability.

Triatholon   8461 Warner Dr.
                                                        Culver City, CA 90230
                                                        (213) 558-3321

From the novice to the elite competitor, *Triatholon* provides a format that is targeted to meet
the needs of nearly every triathlete.

USA Gymnastics   1099 N. Meridian st.
                                                        Indianapolis, IN 46204

The official magazine of the United States Gymnastics Federation accurately captures the preci-
sion and excitement of gymnastics. This colorful and highly recommended publication which
is circulated 6 times a year provides an entertaining, yet informative format on issues and advancements in the sport of gymnastics. ($12.00 per year)

CHAPTER 21

DIRECTORY OF POTENTIAL CONTACTS

Following is a directory of major professional franchises and league offices. It will provide you with addresses and if available, the name of the person to write to so you can inquire as to possible employment or internship openings. With the continuous addition of new leagues and the many new teams on the sporting scene, several of the following franchises may have moved to new headquarters or even ceased their operation by the time you get this list. If the Postal Service returns one of your letters, write to the Commissioner's Office and request the team's new address.

New arenas are springing up across the country and their administrative staffs not only book sporting events, but concerts, circuses, trade shows and many other attractions. Local Chamber of Commerces may provide you with necessary information.

Minor League baseball is the real training ground for the majors and has produced many of the top executives in the sport. Never overlook this route as even though the pay may be minimal, the experience isn't.

This Sports Career Guide and Directory contains much valuable information but is still only a career search helper. Investigate and use your initiative to make contacts. Any one of them could be your starting point.

Now it is up to you. Remember to send out as many personalized letters as possible and talk to as many people as you can. The road to success may be rough, but the rewards can be very satisfying. If you have time, please write us of your success or lack of it in your attempt to enter the world of sports using the techniques we have suggested.

Athletic Achievements
Box 6625
St. Paul, MN 55106
(612) 484-8299

HEAD OFFICES

AMATEUR ORGANIZATIONS

AMATEUR ATHLETIC UNION
3400 W. 86th St.
Indianapolis, IN 46268

INTERNATIONAL OLYMPIC COMMITTEE
Chateau De Vidy
CH-1007
Lausanne, Switzerland

U.S. OLYMPIC COMMITTEE
F. Don Miller - Exec. Dir.
Olympic House
1750 E. Boulder Street
Colorado Springs, Colo. 80909
(303) 632-5551

ARENAS

INTERNATIONAL ASSOCIATION OF
AUDITORIUM MANAGERS
Attn. William Feder
One Illinois Center
111 E. Wacker Drive
Chicago, IL 60601

BASEBALL

OFFICE OF THE COMMISSIONER
Peter Ueberroth
75 Rockefeller Plaza
New York, NY 10019
(212) 371-7800

AMERICAN LEAGUE

Bobby Brown - President
350 Park Avenue
New York, NY 10022
(212) 371-7600

Baltimore Orioles
Edward Bennett Williams - President
Memorial Stadium
Baltimore, MD 21218
(301) 243-9800

Boston Red Sox
Jean R. Yawkey - President
Fenway Park
Boston, MA 02215
(617) 267-9440

California Angels
Gene Autry - President
P.O. Box 2000
Anaheim, CA 92803
(714) 937-6700

Chicago White Sox
Eddie Einhorn - President
Dan Ryan @35th Street
Chicago, IL 60616
(312) 924-1000

Cleveland Indians
Peter Babasi - President
Cleveland Stadium
Cleveland, OH 44114
(216) 861-1200

Detroit Tigers
Jim Campbell - President
2121 Trumbull Avenue
Detroit, MI 48216
(313) 962-4000

Kansas City Royals
Joe Burke - President
P.O. Box 1969
Kansas City, MO 64141
(816) 921-2200

Milwaukee Brewers
Bud Selig - President
Milwaukee County Stadium
Milwaukee, WI 53246
(414) 933-1818

Minnesota Twins
Jerry Bell - President
501 Chicago Avenue South
Minneapolis, MN 55415
(612) 375-1366

New York Yankees
Gene McHale - President
Yankee Stadium
Bronx, NY 10451
(212) 293-4300

Oakland Athletics
Roy Einsenhardt
Oakland Alameda County Coliseum
Oakland, CA 94621
(415) 635-4900

Seattle Mariners
Charles Armstrong - President
P.O. Box 4100
Seattle, WA 98104
(206) 628-3555

Texas Rangers
Michael H. Stone
P.O. Box 1111
Arlington, TX 76010
(817) 273-5222

Toronto Blue Jays
R. Howard Webster - President
P.O. Box 7777, Adelaide St.
Toronto, Ontario M5C 2K7
(416) 595-0077

NATIONAL LEAGUE

Charles Feeney - President
220 Montgomer Street
San Francisco, CA 94104
(212) 371-7300

Atlanta Braves
Ted Turner - President
P.O. Box 4064
Atlanta, GA 30302
(404) 522-7630

Chicago Cubs
Dallas Green - President
1060 West Addison Street
Chicago, IL 60613
(312) 281-5050

Cincinnati Reds
Marge Schott - President
100 Riverfront Stadium
Cincinnati, OH 45202
(513) 421-4510

Houston Astros
Dick Wagner - President
P.O. Box 288
Houstin, TX 77001
(713) 799-9500

Los Angeles Dodgers
Peter O'Malley - President
1000 Elysian Park Avenue
Los Angeles, CA 90012
(213) 224-1500

Montreal Expos
John McHale - President
P.O. Box 500, Station M
Montreal, Quebec H1V 3P2
(514) 253-3434

New York Mets
Fred Wilpon - President
Shea Stadium
Flushing, NY 11368
(212) 507-6387

Philadelphia Phillies
Gill Giles - President
P.O. Box 7575
Philadelphia, PA 19101
(215) 463-6000

Pittsburgh Pirates
MacPrine - President
Three Rivers Stadium
Pittsburgh, PA 15212
(412) 323-5000

St. Louis Cardinals
August Busch, Jr. - President
250 Stadium Plaza
St. Louis, MO 63102
(314) 421-3060

San Diego Padres
Ballard Smith - President
P.O. Box 2000
San Diego, CA 92102
(619) 283-4494

San Francisco Giants
Bob Lurie - President
Candlestick Park
San Francisco, CA 94624
(415) 468-3700

BASEBALL (MINOR LEAGUE)

NATIONAL ASSOCIATION OF
PROFESSIONAL BASEBALL LEAGUES
P.O. Box A
St. Petersburg, FL 33731

American Association
Joe Ryan - President
P.O. Box 382
Wichita, KS 67201

Appalachian League
Chauncey De Vault - President
Box 927
Bristol, VA 24201

California League
Bill Wickert - President
677 Santa Barbara Road
Berkeley, CA 94707

Carolina League
Wallace McKenna - President
Box 1326
Lynchburg, VA 24505

Eastern League
Pat McKernan - President
26 Spadina Parkway
Pittsfield, MA 01201

Florida State League
George MacDonald - President
Box 414
Lakeland, FL 33802

Gulf Coast League
George MacDonald - President
Box 414
Lakeland, FL 33802

Gulf States League
Howard Green - President
1244 Karla Drive
Hurst, TX 76053

International League
George Sisler - President
401 Times Square Bldg.
Rochester, NY 14614

Midwest League
William Walters - President
P.O. Box 444
Burlington, IA 52601

148

New York - Penn League
Vince McNamara - President
220 Brookside Drive
Buffalo, NY 14220

Northwest League
Bob Richmond - President
Box 848
Eugene, OR 97401

Pacific Coast League
Roy Jackson - President
Box 530
Paoli, PA 19301

Pioneer League
Ralph Nelles - President
Box 57
Billings, MT 59103

Southern League
Billy Hitchcock - President
Box 320
Opelika, AL 36801

Texas League
Carl Sawatski - President
Box 5240
Little Rock, AR 72205

Western Carolinas League
John H. Moss - President
Box 49
Kings Mountain, NC 28086

BASKETBALL

NATIONAL BASKETBALL ASSOCIATION
David Stern - Commissioner
645 5th Avenue
New York, NY 10022
(212) 826-7000

Atlanta Hawks
100 Techwood Drive, NW
Atlanta, GA 30303
(404) 681-3600

Boston Celtics
Boston Garden at No. Station
Boston, MA 02114
(617) 623-6050

Chicago Bulls
333 North Michigan Avenue
Chicago, IL 60601
(312) 346-1122

Cleveland Cavaliers
P.O. Box 355
Richfield, OH 4286
(216) 659-9100

Dallas Mavericks
Reunion Arena
777 Sports Street
Dallas, TX 75207

Denver Nuggets
P.O. Box 4286
Denver, CO 80204
(303) 893-6700

Detroit Pistons
Pontiac Silverdome
1200 Featherstone Road
Pontiac, MI 48507
(313) 338-4667

Golden State Warriors
The Oakland Coliseum Arena
Nimitz Freeway & Hegenberger Road
Oakland, CA 94621
(415) 638-6300

Houston Rockets
The Summit
Houston, TX 77046
(713) 627-0600

Indiana Pacers
920 Circle Tower
5 East Market Street
Indianapolis, IN 46204
(317) 632-DUNK

Los Angeles Clippers
L.A. Sports Arena
3939 So. Figueroa St.
Los Angeles, CA 90037
(213) 748-0500

Los Angeles Lakers
P.O. Box 10
Inglewood, CA 90306
(213) 674-6000

Milwaukee Bucks
901 North Fourth Street
Milwaukee, WI 53203
(414) 272-6030

New Jersey Nets
Brendan Byrne Arena
East Rutherford, NJ 07073
(201) 935-8888

New York Knickerbockers
Four Pennsylvania Plaza
New York, NY 10001
(212) 563-8000

Philadelphia 76ers
Veterans Stadium
P.O. Box 25040
Philadelphia, PA 19147
(215) 339-7600

Phoenix Suns
P.O. Box 1369
Phoenix, AZ 85001
(602) 266-5753

Portland Trail Blazers
700 NE Multnomah Street
Suite 950 - Lloyd Building
Portland, OR 97232
(503) 234-9291

San Antonio Spurs
HemisFair Arena
P.O. Box 530
San Antonio, TX 78292
(512) 224-4611

Seattle Supersonics
C-Box 12102
Seattle, WA 98114
(202) 628-8400

Utah Jazz
Salt Palace
100 S.W. Temple
Salt Lake City, UT 84010
(801) 355-5151

Washington Bullets
One Harry S. Truman Drive
Landover, MD 20785
(301) 350-3400

NBA EXPANSION TEAMS

CHARLOTTE
Mr. Max Muhleman
Muhleman Marketing
423 South Sharon Amity Road
Charlotte, North Carolina 28211
(704) 364-2775

ORLANDO
Mr. Pat Williams
Orlondo Profesional Basketball Ltd.
P.O. Box 76
20 North Orange Avenue
Orlondo, Florida 32802
(305) 422-7433

MIAMI
Mr. Lewis Schaffel
The Florida Heat
2980 McFarlane Road
Suite 205
Coconut Grove, Florida 33133
(305) 448-4328

MINNEAPOLIS
Robert A. Stein, Esq.
Minnesota Timberwolves
5525 Cedar Lake Road
Minneapolis, Minnesota 55416
(612) 544-3865

COLLEGE ATHLETICS

National Association of Collegiate
Director of Athletics
Michael J. Cleary - Exec. Dir.
Executive Club West Bldg.
21330 Center Ridge Road
Cleveland, OH 44116

National Collegiate Athletic Association
Exec. Dir.
U.S. Highway 50 & Nall Ave. Box 1906
Shawnee Mission, KA 66222

National Association of Intercollegiate Athletics
Dr. Harry G. Fritz - Exec. Sec.
1205 Baltimore Street
Kansas City, MO 64105

National Junior College Athletic Association
George Killian - Exec. Dir.
12 East 2nd
Hutchinson, KA 67501

National Little College Athletic Association
Del Nobel - Commissioner
P.O. Box 367
Marion, OH 43302

MAJOR COLLEGE CONFERENCES

Atlantic Coast Conference
Robert C. James - Commissioner
P.O. Box 29169
Greensboro, NC 27408

Big Eight Conference
Carl James - Commissioner
600 East 8th Street
Kansas City, MO 64106

Big Sky Conference
John O. Rohning - Commissioner
722 Braemere Road
Boise, Idaho 83702

Big Ten Intercollegiate Conference
Wayne Duke - Commissioner
1111 Plaza Drive - Suite 600
Schaumburg, IL 60159

Central Collegiate Conference
Bob Karnes - Exec. Dir.
Drake University
Des Moines, IA 50311

East Coast Conference
Earnest C. Casale - Commissioner
Temple University
Philadelphia, PA 19122

Eastern College Athletic Conference
Robert M. Whitelaw - Commissioner
P.O. Box 3
Centerville, MA 02632

Ivey League Athletic Conference
304 Elm Club
Princeton University
Princeton, NJ 08540

Metropolitan Collegiate Athletic Conference
Steve Natchell - Commissioner
229 Peachtree NE
Cain Tower 2300
Atlanta, GA 30303

Mid-American Athletic Conference
Jim Lessig- Commissioner
4 Seagate
Suite 501
Toledo, OH 43604

Mid-Eastern Athletic Conference
Earl Mason - Commissioner
P.O. Box 1087
Durham, NC

Midwestern Collegiate Conference
Jim Shaffer Commissioner
1099 N. Meridian
Suite 642
Indianapolis, IN 46204

Missouri Valley Conference
James Hancy - Commissioner
200 N. Broadway
Suite 1905
St. Louis, MO 63102

Ohio Valley Conference
Robert Vanatta - Commissioner
1025 Dove Run Road
Suite 106
Lexington, KY

Pacific Coast Athletic Association
Jesse T. Hill - Commissioner
9800 S. Sepulveda Blvd.
Suite 820
Los Angeles, CA 90045

Pacific 10 Conference
Thomas Hansen - Exec. Dir.
800 S. Broadway - Suite 400
Walnut Creek, CO 94546

Southeastern Athletic Conference
H. Boyd McWhorter - Commissioner
1214 Central Bank Bldg.
Birmingham, AL 35233

Southern Conference
Dave Hart - Commissioner
No. 5 Woodlawn Green
Suite 106
Charlotte, NC 28210

Southwest Athletic Conference
Fred Jacoby - Commissioner
1300 W. Mockingbird Ln. S-444
Dallas, TX 47420

Sun Belt Conference
Vic Bubas - Commissioners
1408 N. Westshore Blvd.
Suite 1010
Tampa, FL 33607

West Coast Athletic Conference
Michael Gilleran
5421 Geary Blvd.
San Francisco, CA 94121

Western Athletic Conference
Joseph Kearney
14 W. Dry Creek
Littleton, CO 80120

FOOTBALL

The National Football League
Pete Rozelle - Commissioner
410 Park Avenue
New York, NY 10022
(212) 223-3930
(212) 758-1500

AMERICAN FOOTBALL CONFERENCE

Buffalo Bills
One Bills Drive
Orchard Park, NY 14127
(716) 648-1800

Cincinnati Bengals
200 Riverfront Stadium
Cincinnati, OH 45202
(513) 621-3550

Cleveland Browns
434 Eastland Road
Berea, OH 44017
(216) 696-5555

Denver Broncos
5700 Logan Street
Denver, CO 80216
(303) 296-1982

Houston Oilers
P.O. Box 1516
Houston, TX 77001
(713) 797-9111

Indianapolis Colts
4900 Kessler Blvd., East
Indianapolis, IN 46220
(317) 252-2658

Kansas City Chiefs
One Arrowhead Drive
Kansas City, MO 64129
(816) 924-9300

Los Angeles Raiders
332 Center Street
El Segundo, CA 90245
(213) 322-3451

Miami Dolphins
2550 Biscayne Blvd.
Miami, FL 33137
(305) 576-1000

New England Patriots
Schaefer Stadium - Rte. 1
Foxboro, MA 02035
(616) 543-7911

New York Jets
598 Madison Avenue
New York, NY 10022
(212) 421-6600
or practice: (516) 538-6600

Pittsburgh Steelers
Three Rivers Stadium
300 Stadium Circle
Pittsburgh, PA
(412) 323-1200

San Diego Chargers
San Diego Stadium
P.O. Box 20666
San Diego, CA 92120
(619) 280-2122

Seattle Seahawks
5305 Lake Washington Blvd.
Kirkland, WA 98033
(206) 827-9777

NATIONAL FOOTBALL CONFERENCE

Atlanta Falcons
Suwanee Road at 1-85
Suwanee, GA 30174
(404) 588-1111

Chicago Bears
55 East ackson
Chicago, IL 60604
P.O. Box 204
Lake Forest, IL 60045
Administration (312) 663-5100
PR, Personnel (312) 295-6600

Dallas Cowboys
6116 North Central Express
Dallas, TX 75206
(214) 369-8000

Detroit Lions
1200 Featherstone
P.O. Box 4200
Pontiac, MI 48057
(313) 335-4131

Green Bay Packers
1265 Lombardi Avenue
Green Bay, WI 54303
(414) 494-2351

Los Angeles Rams
2327 Lincoln Drive
Anaheim, CA 92801
(714) 535-7267

Minnesota Vikings
9520 Viking Drive
Eden Prairie, MN 55344
(612) 828-6500

New Orleans Saints
1500 Podyras Street
New Orleans, LA
(504) 587-3034

New York Giants
Giants Stadium
East Rutherford, NJ 07073
(201) 463-2600

Philadelphia Eagles
Broad St. & Patterson Ave.
Philadelphia, PA 19148
(215) 421-0777

San Francisco 49ers
711 Nevada Street
Redwood City, CA 94061
(415) 365-3420

Tampa Bay Buccaneers
One Buccaneer Place
Tampa Bay, FL 33607
(813) 870-2700

Washington Redskins
P.O. Box 17247
Dulles International Airport
Washington, DC 2004
(703) 471-9100

CANADIAN FOOTBALL LEAGUE

J.G. Gaudaur - Commissioner
1 Bala Plaza - Suite 415
Bala CYNWYD, PA 19004

B.C. Lions Football Club
Bob Ackles - General Manager
550 Burrard Street
Vancouver, B.C. V6C 2J6

Calgary Stampeder Football Club
Joe Tiller - General Manger
McMahon Stadium
Box 3957 - Stadium B
Calgary, Alberta T2M 4M5

Edmonton Eskimo Football Club
Norm Kimball - General Manager
11820 Kingsway Avenue
Edmonton, Alberta T5G 0X5

Hamilton Tiger-Cat Football Club
Ralph Sazio - President
Box 172
Hamilton, Ontario L8N 3A2

Ottawa Rough Rider Football Club
Frank Clair - General Manager
Lansdowne Park
Ottawa, Ontario K1S 3W7

Saskatchewan Roughrider Football Club
Ken Preston - General Manager
3418 Hill Avenue
Regina, Saskatchewan S4S 0W9

Toronto Argonaut Football Club
Dick Shatto - General Manager
655 Dixon Road Unit 52
Rexdale, Ontario M9W 1J4

Winnipeg Blue Bomber Football Club
Earl Lunsford - General Manager
1465 Maroons Road
Winnipeg, Manitoba R3G 0L6

HOCKEY

The National Hockey League
Clarence Campbell - Commissioner
920 Sun Life Building
Montreal, Canada H3B 2W2

Boston Bruins
Boston Garden
150 Causeway Street
Boston MA 02114

Buffalo Sabres
Memorial Auditorium
140 Main Street
Buffalo, NY 14202
(716) 856-7300

Calgary Flames
P.O. Box 1540
Station "M"
Calgary, Alberta T2P 3B9

Chicago Black Hawks
Chicago Stadium
1800 West Madison Street
Chicago, IL 60612

Detroit Red Wings
Joe Louis Sports Arena
600 Civic Center Drive
Detroit, MI 48226

Edmonton Oilers
Northlands Coliseum
7424-118 Avenue
Edmonton, Alberta T5B 4M9

Hartford Whalers
One Civic Center Plaza
Hartford, CN 06103

Los Angeles Kings
The Forum
3900 West Manchester Blvd.
Inglewood, CA 90306

Minnesota North Stars
Met Center
7901 Cedar Avenue South
Bloomington, MN 55420

Montreal Canadians
The Forum
2313 St. Catherine St., West
Montreal, Quebec H3H 1N2

New Jersey Devils
Byrne Meadowlands Arena
P.O. Box 504
East Rutherford, NJ 07033

New York Islanders
Nassau Veterans Mem. Coliseum
Uniondale, NY 15533

New York Rangers
Madison Square Garden
4 Pennsylvania Plaza
New York, NY 10001

Philadelphia Flyers
The Spectrum
Pattison Place
Philadelphia, PA 19148

Pittsburgh Penguins
Civic Arena
Pittsburgh, PA 15219

Quebec Nordiques
Colisee de Quebec
2205 Avenue du Colisee
Quebec, Que G1L 4W7

St. Louis Blues
The Checkerdome
5700 Oakland Avenue
St. Louis, MO 63110

Toronto Maple Leafs
Maple Leaf Gardens
60 Carlton Street
Toronto, Ontario M5B 1L1

Vancouver Canucks
Pacific Coliseum
100 North Renfrew St.
Vancouver, B.C. V5K 3N7

Washington Capitals
Capital Center
Landover, MD 20786

Winnipeg Jets
Winnipeg Arena
15-1430 Maroons Road
Winnipeg, Manitoba R3G 0L5

AMERICAN HOCKEY LEAGUE
31 Elm Street #533
Springfield, MN 01103
(413) 781-2030

CENTRAL HOCKEY LEAGUE
6060 N. Central Express #178
Dallas, TX 75206
(214) 697-8585

SOCCER

MAJOR INDOOR SOCCER LEAGUE
Earl M. Foreman - Commissioner
1 Bala Plaza - Suite 415
Bala Cywyd, PA 19004
(215) 667-4290

Baltimore Blast
Civic Center
201 W. Baltimore Street
Baltimore, MD 21201
(301) 528-0100

Chicago Sting
425 N. Michigan Avenue
Suite 777
Chicago, IL 60611
(312) 245-5444

Cleveland Force
34555 Chagrin Blvd.
Moreland Hills, OH 44022
(216) 247-4740

Minnesota Strikers
8100 Cedar Avenue South
Suite 115
Bloomington, MN 55420
(612) 854-3616

St. Louis Steamers
212 N. Kirkwood
St. Louis, MO 63122
(314) 821-1111

Dallas Sidekicks
Reunion Arena
777 Sports Steet
Dallas, TX 75207
(214) 760-7330

Kansas City Comets
Kemper Arena
1800 Genessee Street
Kansas, City, MO 64102
(816) 421-7770

Los Angeles Lazers
The Forum
P.O. Box 10
Inglewood, CA 90306
(213) 419-3179

San Diego Sockers
San Diego Sports Arena
3500 Sports Arena Blvd.
San Diego, CA 92110
(619) 224-4625

Tacoma Stars
CS 2267 - 1121 A Street
Tacoma, WA 98401
(206) 627-8474

Wichita Wings
114 South Broadway
Wichita, KS 67202
(316) 262-3545

SPORTS AND ATHLETIC ORGANIZATIONS

The following organizations can offer information concerning the sport or activity with which they are associated. Many will be able to provide dates of contests, requirements for certain jobs, and additional sources of information.

NATIONAL ARCHERY ASSOCIATION
OF THE UNITED STATES
1951 Geraldson Drive
Lancaster, PA 17601

COLLEGE ATHLETIC BUSINESS
MANAGERS ASSOCIATION
University of Iowa
Iowa City, IA 52242

AMERICAN AMATEUR BASEBALL CONGRESS
2855 West Market Street
Akron, OH 44313

AMERICAN ASSOCIATION OF
COLLEGE BASEBALL COACHES
123 Assembly Hall
Champaign, IL 61820

ASSOCIATION OF PROFESSIONAL
BALL PLAYERS OF AMERICA
530 East Wardlow Road - Suite 4
Long Beach, CA 90807

NATIONAL ASSOCIATION OF LEAGUES,
UMPIRES AND SCORERS
Box 1420
Wichita, KS 67201

NATIONAL ASSOCIATION OF
PROFESSIONAL BASEBALL LEAGUES
P.O. Box A
225 Fourth Street South
St. Petersburg, FL 33731

NATIONAL BASEBALL CONGRESS
Box 1420
Wichita, KS 67201

INTERNATIONAL ASSOCIATION OF
APPROVED BASKETBALL OFFICIALS
1620 Dual Highway East
Hagerstown, MD 21740

NATIONAL ASSOCIATION OF BASKETBALL
COACHES OF THE UNITED STATES
18 Orchard Avenue
Branford, CT 06405

AMERICAN BILLIARD ASSOCIATION
1660 Lin Lor Court
Elgin, IL 60120

NATIONAL CHEERLEADING FOUNDATION
7800 Conser Place
Overland Park, KS 66204

NATIONAL CHEERLEADING ASSOCIATION
9150 Markville
Dallas, TX 75238

NATIONAL HIGH SCHOOL
COACHES ASSOCIATION
3423 East Silver Springs Blvd., Suite 9
Ocala, FL 32670

SPORT FISHING INSTITUTE
608 13th Street NW
Washington, DC 20005

AMERICAN FOOTBALL COACHES ASSOCIATION
Box 8705
Durham, NC 27707

FOOTBALL WRITERS ASSOCIATION OF AMERICA
Box 1022
Edmond, OK 73034

NATIONAL FOOTBALL FOUNDATION
  AND HALL OF FAME
201 East 42nd Street, Suite 1506
New York, NY 10017

POP WARNER JUNIOR LEAGUE FOOTBALL
1315 Walnut Street, Suite 606
Philadelphia, PA 19107

PROFESSIONAL FOOTBALL WRITERS OF AMERICA
6210 Quay Street
Arvada, CO 80003

GOLF COACHES ASSOCIATION OF AMERICA
Ohio Wesleyan University
Deleware, OH 43015

GOLF WRITERS ASSOCIATION OF AMERICA
1720 Section Road - Suite 210
Cincinnatti, OH 45237

NATIONAL ASSOCIATION OF COLLEGIATE
  GYMNASTICS COACHES
c/o Athletic Department
Houston Baptist University
Houston, TX 77074

AMERICAN ATHLETIC ASSOCIATION FOR THE DEAF
3916 Lantern Drive
Silver Spring, MD 20902

INTERNATIONAL COMMITTEE OF THE SILENT SPORTS
(handicapped)
Gallaudet College
Washington, DC 20002

NATIONAL HANDICAPPED SPORTS
  AND RECREATION ASSOCIATION
4105 East Florida Avenue - Third Floor
Denver, CO 80222

NAITONAL WHEELCHAIR BASKETBALL ASSOCIATION
110 Seaton Bldg.
University of Kentucky
Lexington, KY 40506

SPECIAL OLYMPICS (handicapped)
1701 K Street NW - Suite 203
Washington, DC 20006

AMATEUR HOCKEY ASSOCIATION
  OF THE UNITED STATES
10 Lake Circle
Colorado, Springs, CO 80906

AMERICAN HOCKEY LEAGUE
31 Elm Street - suite 533
Springfield, MA 01103

NATIONAL HOCKEY LEAGUE
920 Sun Life Bldg.
Montreal, PQ, Canada H3B 2W2

AMERICAN TRAINERS ASSOCIATION
7805 Ruxway Road
Baltimore, MD 21204

THOROUGHBRED CLUB OF AMERICA
P.O. Box 8147
Lexington, KY 40503

UNITED STATES HARNESS
  WRITERS' ASSOCIATION (horse racing)
P.O. Box 10
Batavia, NY 14020

UNITED STATES THOROUGHBRED
  TRAINERS OF AMERICA
19363 James Couzens Highway
Detroit, MI 48235

UNITED STATES AMATEUR JAI ALAI
  PLAYERS ASSOCIATION
100 SE Second Avenue
Miami, FL 33131

UNITED STATES COMMITTEE-
  SPORTS FOR ISREAL
130 E. 59th Street
New York, NY 10022

THE LACROSSE FOUNDATION
Newton H. White Jr. Athletic Center
Homewood
Baltimore, MD 21218

UNITED STATES OLYMPIC COMMITTEE
57 Park Avenue
New York, NY 10016

NATIONAL PADDLEBALL ASSOCIATION
North Campus Recreation Bldg.
University of Michigan
Ann Arbor, MI 48105

UNITED STATES MODERN PENTATHLON
  AND BIATHLON ASSOCIATION
707 E. Broad Street
Falls Church, VA 22046

PEOPLE-TO-PEOPLE SPORTS COMMITTEE
98 Cutter Mill Road
Great Neck, NY 11021

NORTH AMERICAN SOCIETY FOR THE
  PSYCHOLOGY OF SPORT
    AND PHYSICAL ACTIVITY
Hutchinson Hall DX-10
University of Washington
Seattle, WA 98195

COLLEGE SPORTS INFORMATION
  DIRECTORS OF AMERICA
University of Wisconsin - Parkside
Kenosha, WI 53141

AMERICAN SKI TEACHERS
  ASSOCIATION OF NATUR TEKNIK
Camelback Ski Area
Tannersville, PA 18372

INTERNATIONAL SKI WRITERS ASSOCIATION
Rheintalweg 106
CH-4125 Riehen, Switzerland

PROFESSIONAL SKI INSTRUCTORS
  OF AMERICA
1726 Champa
Denver, CO 80202

UNITED STATES SKI WRITERS ASSOCIATION
7 Kensington Road
Glen Falls, NY 12801

NATIONAL INTERCOLLEGIATE SOCCER
OFFICIALS ASSOCIATION
131 Moffitt Boulevard
Islip, NY 11751

NATIONAL SOCCER COACHES ASSOCIATION
OF AMERICA
668 La Vista Road
Walnut Creek, CA 94598

NORTH AMERICAN SOCCER LEAGUE
(League temporarily suspended)
1133 Ave. of the Americas
New York, NY 10036

NATIONAL ACADEMY OF SPORTS
220 E. 63rd Street
New York, NY 10021

ASSOCIATION OF SPORTS MUSEUMS
AND HALLS OF FAME
Citizens Savings Athletic Foundation
9800 S. Sepulveda Blvd.
Los Angeles, CA 90045

AMERICAN SWIMMING COACHES ASSOCIATION
1 Hall of Fame Drive
Ft. Lauderdale, FL 33316

INTERCOLLEGIATE TENNIS COACHES
ASSOCIATION
Michigan State University
East Lansing, MI 48824

LAWN TENNIS WRITERS' ASSOCIATION
OF AMERICA
Sports Department, Washington Post
1150 15th Street NW
Washington, DC 20005

UNITED STATES PROFESSIONAL TENNIS
ASSOCIATION
6701 Highway 58
Harrison, TN 37341

UNITED STATES TRACK COACHES ASSOCIATION
745 State Circle
Ann Arbor, MI 48104

UNITED STATES TRACK AND FIELD
ASSOCIATION
30 N. Norton Avenue
Tucson, AZ 85719

AMERICAN GUIDES ASSOCIATION (trail)
Box B Woodland, CA 95695

NATIONAL ATHLETIC TRAINERS ASSOCIATION
c/o Philadelphia Eagles
Veterans Stadium
Philadelphia, PA 19148

MAJOR LEAGUE UMPIRES ASSOCIATION
450 W. 14th Street
Chicago Heights, IL 60411

PROFESSIONAL ASSOCIATION OF DIVING
INSTRUCTORS
2064 N. Bush Street
Santa Ana, CA 92706

UNITED STATES VOLLEYBALL ASSOCIATION
557 4th Street
San Francisco, CA 94107

NATIONAL WRESTLING COACHES
ASSOCIATION
c/o Athletic Department
University of Utah
Salt Lake City, UT 84112

SPORTS MUSEUMS AND HALLS OF FAME

Many fine sports museums and halls of fame exist in this country and Canada. A visit to some of them provides an excellent opportunity to expand your knowledge of a sport that interests you.

AQUATIC HALL OF FAME AND MUSEUM
OF CANADA, INC.
c/o 436 Main Street
Winnipeg, Manitoba, Canada R3B 1B2

AUTO RACING HALL OF FAME
4790 West 16th Street
Speedway, IN 46224

BERMUDA SPORTS HALL OF FAME
Box 121
Hamilton, Bermuda

BOSTON MUSEUM OF SPORTS
89 Franklin Street - Suite 2000
Boston, MA 02110

BRITISH COLUMBIA SPORTS HALL OF
FAME AND MUSEUM
P.O. Box 69020 - Station "K"
Vancouver, B.C.
Canada V5K 4W3

CANADA'S SPORTS HALL OF FAME
Exhitition Place
Toronto, Canada M6K 3C3

CANADIAN FOOTBALL HALL OF FAME
58 Jackson Street West
Hamilton, Ontario, Canada L8P 1L4

CANADIAN LACROSSE HALL OF FAME
1807 Hamilton Street
New Westminster, B.C.
Canada V3M 2P3

COLLEGE FOOTBALL HALL OF FAME
P.O. Box 300
Kings Mills, OH 45034

DELAWARE SPORTS HALL OF FAME
News Journal Papers
833 Orange Street
Wilmington, DE 19802

FLORIDA SPORTS HALL OF FAME
P.O. Box 1
Cypress Gardens, FL 33880

GREATER CLEVELAND SPORTS HALL OF
  FAME FOUNDATION, INC.
1375 Euclid Avenue - Suite 412
Cleveland, OH 44115

GREEN BAY PACKER HALL OF FAME
1901 South Oneida
Green Bay, WI 54303

GREYHOUND HALL OF FAME
407 South Buckeye
Abilene, KS 67410

HALL OF FAME OF THE TROTTER
240 Main Street
Goshen, NY 10924

HOCKEY HALL OF FAME
Exhibition Place
Toronto, Ontario
Canada M6K 3C3

INTERNATIONAL HOCKEY HALL OF FAME
  AND MUSEUM
303 York Street, Box 82
Kingston, Ontario
Canada

INTERNATIONAL PALACE OF SPORTS, INC.
Camelot Square
North Webster, IN 46555

INTERNATIONAL SOFTBALL CONGRESS
  HALL OF FAME
9800 S. Sepulveda Blvd.
Los Angeles, CA 90045

INTERNATIONAL SWIMMING HALL OF FAME
One Hall of Fame Drive
Fort Lauderdale, FL 33316

INTERNATIONAL TENNIS HALL OF FAME
  AND TENNIS MUSEUM
194 Bellevue Avenue
Newport, RI 02840

LACROSSE FOUNDATION, INC. AND
  LACROSSE HALL OF FAME
Newton H. White Athletic Center
Homewood, MD 21218

NAISMITH MEMORIAL BASKETBALL
  HALL OF FAME
460 Alden Street
Springfield, MA 01109

NATIONAL BOWLING HALL OF FAME
  AND MUSEUM, INC.
5301 South 76th Street
Greendale, WI 53129

NATIONAL COWBOY HALL OF FAME
1700 N.E. 63rd Street
Oklahoma City, OK 73111

NATIONAL FOOTBALL FOUNDATION AND
  HALL OF FAME, INC.
201 East 42nd Street - Suite 1506
New York, NY 10017

NATIONAL FOOTBALL FOUNDATION
  HALL OF FAME
P.O. Box 300
Kings Mills, OH 45034

NATIONAL FRESH WATER FISHING
  HALL OF FAME, INC.
Box 33 - Wisconsic Avenue
Hayward, WI 54843

NATIONAL POLISH-AMERICAN SPORTS
  HALL OF FAME AND MUSEUM
c/o 9131 Grayfield Avenue
Detroit, MI 48239

NATIONAL SKI HALL OF FAME
Box 191
Ishpeming, MI 49849

NATIONAL SOARING MUSEUM, INC.
Harris Hill, R.D. No. 1
Elmira, NY 14903

NATIONAL SOFTBALL HALL OF
  FAME AND MUSEUM
2801 N.E. 50th Street
Oklahoma City, OK 73111

NATIONAL TRACK AND FIELD HALL OF
  FAME OF THE U.S.A.
1524 Kanawha Blvd., East
Charleston, WV 25311

NATIONAL WRESTLING HALL OF FAME
405 West Hall of Fame Avenue
Stillwater, OK 74074

NEWFOUNDLAND SPORTS HALL OF FAME
Rm. 18 Colonial Building
Military Road
St. John's Newfoundland
Canada A1C 2C9

NEW BRUNSWICK SPORTS HALL OF FAME
Queen Street, P.O. Box 6000
Fredericton, New Brunswick E3B 5H1

NORTH CAROLINA SPORTS
  HALL OF FAME
P.O. Box 385
Raliegh, NC 27602

PRO FOOTBALL HALL OF FAME
2121 Harrison Avenue, N.W.
Canton, OH 44708

ST. LOUIS SPORTS HALL OF FAME, INC.
100 Stadium Plaza
St. Louis, MO 63102

SAN DIEGO HALL OF CHAMPIONS, INC.
1439 El Prado, Balboa Park
San Diego, cA 92101

SASKATCHEWAN SPORTS
  HALL OF FAME
1915 South Railway
Regina, Saskatchewan
Canada S4P 0B1

SPORT NOVA SCOTIA HALL OF FAME
P.O. Box 3010 S.
Halifax, Nova Scotia
Canada B3J 3G6

STATE OF MICHIGAN SPORTS
  HALL OF FAME
c/o 1010 Joanne Court
Bloomfield Hills, MI 48013

TEXAS SPORTS HALL OF FAME,
  FOUNDATION
601 Fidelity Union Life Building
Dallas, TX 75201

UNITED STATES FIGURE SKATING
  ASSOCIATION HALL OF FAME
Sears Crescent Building - Suite 500
Boston, MA 02108

UNITED STATES HOCKEY
  HALL OF FAME, INC.
Eveleth, MN 55734

UNITED STATES TRACK AND
  FIELD HALL OF FAME
P.O. Box 297
Angola, In 46703

WORLD GOLF HALL OF FAME
P.O. Box 1908
Pinehurst, NC 28374